THE MUFFIN CHRONICLES

JUDE BALES

Cover Photo & Cover Design – Vincent Bales
Author Photo – Terry Bales
Publishing Coordinator – Sharon Kizziah-Holmes

INDIE PUB PRESS

Indie Pub Press
Springfield, Missouri
Printed in the United States of America

ISBN -13: 978-1-964559-64-3

DEDICATION

For the love of Muffin.

TABLE OF CONTENTS

ACKNOWLEDGMENTS

I would like to thank my husband Terry for all of his help in putting this book together, plus for all of the many times that he read The Muffin Chronicles after I would do another re-write.

Much gratitude to our son Vincent for his advice, editing help, reading of the manuscript and all-around tech help.

Thanks also to our daughter Becky and her husband Abe along with our two granddaughters, Ambria and Alice, for listening to excerpts of The Muffin Chronicles and sharing their thoughts.

I would like to thank my dear friend and retired English teacher Connie Frankenfield for reading the manuscript and giving lots of wonderful advice and encouragement.

Many heartfelt thanks to Sharon Kizziah-Holmes at Paperback Press for all she does for first-time authors publishing their first book. A dream come true!

Thanks to all of you.

PROLOGUE

IN THE BEGINNING

I t was the golden haze of the sunlight that first woke her that morning. Then it was her built in feline intuition that had this little gray Cat rising up with eyes closely scanning the alley in which she was in. Living mostly outside she was always alert for enemy cats and dogs too, in the westside neighborhood she thought of as home.

Looking further afield her eyes connected with those of another cat. A larger and obviously male black cat by the way he was flaunting himself. Her eyes never leaving his, she studied his position. Then with no hesitation whatsoever this beautiful gray Cat went headlong into battle with this too conceited and overgrown black male cat.

She never waited when there was a challenge from other felines. No this Warrior Cat always began the fight on her own terms. His eyes widening the enemy cat was about to take his stance, as the little gray Cat took a running leap crashing into him sideways!

Landing deftly on her feet she watched as her opponent went rolling. Her calculations being correct she smiled a satisfied Cat's smile as the enemy cat landed hard up against several old trash cans. The black cat was so dazed that before he could rise the trash cans teetering wildly collapsed on top of him. Never one to kick someone when they were down, this amazing little gray Cat turned and walked away, leaving the enemy black cat to sort himself out.

Shaking off this early morning experience, the little gray Cat roamed around the neighborhood on the westside in true gypsy fashion. Being a peace loving Cat by nature, she only done battles with other cats when challenged. Sighing to herself, she wished for humans to call her own. For though this gypsy Cat had met many friendly humans while roaming the westside neighborhood, she had yet to find any who recognized her for the true Warrior Cat that she was.

The little gray Cat had almost despaired of ever finding some true kindred spirits and maybe a home in which a bit of comfort could be found. Then one day as she was out for a stroll on Lexington Avenue, she noticed that the pretty faded green house with the invitingly large front porch was no longer vacant. There were cars in the driveway and comfy looking chairs on the porch.

She began to hang out cautiously in the front yard so as to try to catch a glimpse of the humans that lived there, for inexplicably she was drawn to them it seemed. Over the period of a couple of weeks the little gray Cat became most familiar with those that lived there. Her feline intuition told her that they were different from the other humans she had encountered. Here just might be the home this little gray Cat was looking for. Venturing closer and closer to the faded green house until one day she climbed the steps and was on the front porch itself!

This story is told in many layers and on many levels. But the one thing that will always remain the same is the never ending love that they all have for one another...

LEXINGTON AVENUE

I t was a busy cool December day for the new family
moving into the pretty faded green house on
Lexington Avenue. Unloading their belongings
from the U-Haul the three began arranging furniture,
unboxing dishes, hanging their clothes in closets and
all the many other tasks of setting up house. The
westside neighborhood seemed be a friendly one and
for that this family was very grateful.

They settled into their new home with Christmas
upon them. Once decorated for the holiday, they fixed
turkey with all of trimmings for their first Christmas
in the faded green house. It was enjoyed immensely
by all with much turkey and holiday fare leftover.

Long about this time a very pretty gray Cat was
noticed out in the front yard. At times this friendly Cat
was even seen on the front porch. The family
wondered if the kitty was without home or maybe was
just out visiting the neighbors.

Finally she as we discovered her to be, came so

regularly that the family whose names were Vincent, Mum and Pops decided she should just live with them. So it came to pass that this little gray Cat became a member of their family and Vincent named her Muffin!

Muffin had been living with her family for a couple of months. She came and went as she pleased in true gypsy fashion, for she had adopted Vincent, Mum and Pops as much as they had adopted her. So she moved about with free will and a very happy Muffin she was too.

One day as Vincent, Mum and Pops were enjoying a meal together, Vincent all of a sudden out of the blue says "Ok it was me, I fed Muffin turkey when she came up to the porch. So she kept coming back."

Mum and Pops were like "Oh well that would explain why she kept coming to visit us. Thank you Vincent for finding us such an awesome fat little gray Cat!" For we all loved Muffin dearly.

Muffin, who had been eating her meal along side of them, walked over to rub against Vincent's leg as if to say "Oh, so you finally decided to tell Mum and Pops our little secret huh?"

Although Vincent moved away from our place on Lexington Avenue a few months later to strike out on his own, he came back to our faded green house often to visit with us and play with The Muffin, as we had nicknamed her. Muffin being a Cat of much character, very much enjoyed these visits. Being intelligent enough to know that Vincent wanted to see her as much as he wanted to see Mum and Pops. Muffin, looking around the room at her people would smile a Cat's smile, totally content to have her three favorite humans all in one place.

Muffin we discovered was a very possessive Cat too and would not allow another cat into our yard.

Instead she would give the intruder a menacing look of Warrior Cat warning and proceed to run them right back out of the yard. "Who did they think they were anyway? This was her family!" We were finding out more and more what a true Warrior our little gray Cat was!

Having never lived inside a house before Muffin had much to learn. Like not realizing that furniture might sometimes be moved or a yoga mat could suddenly appear on the living room floor. Upon seeing something new she would freeze going into high alert when this happened, then approach these seemly foreign objects with caution thinking there was an intruder. But no it was just Mum and Pops pulling their shenanigans again. Whew! Eventually she became used to these types of things. We for our part were amazed by Muffin's stealth in action. She was truly one of a kind!

Being a very versatile Cat, she loved to stretch and roll around while Mum did her yoga routine in the living room. Muffin considered this part of her physical fitness program for staying in tiptop shape for when doing battles with other cats.

Not having been around music before it took Muffin awhile to really enjoy Mum and Pops practicing for gigs. She soon became a huge fan though and showed up regularly to listen. She really liked the one about the stray cat strut. Meow! That one was right up her alley.

Sadly the westside neighborhood diminished a couple of years later and Muffin found herself doing battles with enemy cats more and more often. Mum and Pops also had to pay more close attention to who was driving or walking by in the neighborhood. Gunshots were even heard at times. Muffin thought she might have to step in and help Mum and Pops do battle with some of these unsavory humans. They all began to realize they were going to have to sell their faded green house and leave the westside neighborhood. None of them felt like they even had a choice. So it was decided that like Vincent, the three of them were supposed to move on to adventures elsewhere. Talks were had with Vincent being present at these meetings. Mum and Pops weren't sure what they were going to do next and wanted to keep their options open. Vincent after talking to his roommate Brenden said that Muffin could come live with him at his apartment on Campbell Avenue. So with the close of the house on Lexington Avenue looming, Muffin moved in with Vincent and Brenden. She quite enjoyed riding in the car with Vincent over to his apartment she discovered!

ROOMMATES

Arriving at his place on Campbell Avenue, Vincent with Muffin in toll climbed the stairs to his apartment. As he brought her inside, she avidly took in the space in which she would be living. Sitting Muffin down near the kitchen, Vincent smiling said he would be right back with her things. Returning he set up all of her belongings and gave her the grand tour of the place. Muffin really liked Vincent and Brenden's style and she noticed there were a couple of windows that would be great for sightseeing! She was to meet Brenden when he returned later. Vincent and her really enjoyed one another's company and had a huge love for each other as well. Wow! With her new digs to explore Muffin knew there would be many wild cat adventures with Vincent and Brenden!

Mum and Pops with the sale of their house on Lexington Avenue, had outfitted their Jeep with only their most needful belongings for travel. Having the bulk of their things put in storage while they explored their options, they would remain without home for many months letting their wandering take them wherever they may go.

Four weeks later Vincent, Mum and Pops flew to Ireland. A trip they had always dreamed of, ten days of Irish bliss! Having carefully planned for Muffin's care and comfort while they were away, this would give Muffin and Brenden some time to really get to know one another.

Returning from their holiday in beautiful Ireland, Vincent, Mum and Pops walked into the apartment still floating on a wisp of an Irish dream. They lavished The Muffin with attention and thanked Brenden profusely for tending to her while they were away. Muffin, overjoyed to see her three favorite humans rubbed against their legs and purred loudly!

After returning from Ireland, Vincent settled back into his routine with Muffin and Brenden. While Mum and Pops deciding they needed something to drive that they could sleep in the back of, bought a chevy van from her brother Scott. Customizing the interior and adding a bed they then were more able to have a home on wheels for travel. It also allowed them to camp at their daughter Becky's place too. Sometime Mum and Pops would spend a night with Vincent, Muffin and Brenden. It gave them all some hang out time together. Plus Muffin visitation was a real thing and always very much looked forward too, just as Vincent had come to visit her on Lexington Avenue. Muffin liked to show Mum and Pops tricks she had learned while living this new apartment life. A good time was had by all with many stories being told!

After several months of travel, Mum and Pops came across a mobile home for sale. It was very close to Table Rock Lake, which was nice. Thinking with buying it cheap that they would fix the home up and live there, it seemed like a good idea at the time. The only problem was that Mum and Pops soon discovered they didn't like the place, it just didn't feel right. Besides it was harder to see The Muffin and Vincent while fixing up a mobile home. Thankfully with little money invested in the place, Mum and Pops were able to sell the home in record time. Yay! Muffin and Vincent were happy to see them more often again. For they had worried about Mum and Pops working so hard on that place.

Another month went by with the four of them seeing each other whenever they could as Mum and Pops roamed about in their chevy van. Then one day a place not far from Vincent and Muffin came up for sell. After careful consideration Mum and Pops bought the place. Now once again they were close and would be able to visit them more often. Mum went back to work at The Walnut Street Inn, a lovely Bed and Breakfast in the area. Pops started work at a cabinet shop near their new place. They went often to see Vincent, Muffin and Brenden at their apartment on Campbell Avenue. They even got to know Brenden's girlfriend, Madison. They always had a great time and also helped care for The Muffin if the guys were extra busy.

Throughout the time of Vincent and Brenden sharing an apartment. There was the knowledge that at the end of the lease they would each get their own apartments. Brenden and his girlfriend Madison were going to be married in October, so both planned to get their own apartment in mid-September. We knew we would miss seeing Brenden and Madison as well.

Mid-September moving day came with Vincent and Muffin moving to their apartment on Walnut Street, while Brenden and Madison moved to their apartment on Weller Street. Vincent, Mum and Pops would be attending their wedding in October and looked forward to it. This was Vincent's first ever on his own apartment. Everyone agreed that having Muffin there with him could only make the experience better! She for her part was totally excited about the car ride to their new place and getting Vincent all to herself to hang out with!

Mum and Pops helped them move their belongings into their apartment on Walnut Street. Once inside of it, Muffin prowled around exploring it from top to bottom. She quickly decided that she loved the place and it had many cool spots where she could hang out. The second floor windows were great for her to lounge in, as was the tall chairs in the kitchen. She was equally happy lying on Vincent's bed with him or chilling with him on his dog bed sofa watching one of his favorite shows, "Breaking Bad". She even liked his big bathroom, lots of stuff to check out in there! Probably the only thing Muffin didn't like about the bathroom was the bathtub Vincent occasionally gave her a bath in. This The Muffin did not like! Although she did feel ever so much better afterward. Plus her fur was very silky and clean too. Making her feel even more like the queen of her castle.

While living at the apartment on Walnut Street in downtown Springfield, Vincent worked a night shift, sleeping during the daytime. Muffin was overjoyed to see that one of her humans had finally learned to sleep on Cat time. She wondered if maybe now Vincent would developed some real fur and have a more Catlike appearance, he he...

Mum and Pops loved to go visit Vincent and Muffin on Walnut Street. They would come over right before Vincent would be waking up for work. Upon arrival Muffin would greet them at the door. Then after putting the tea kettle on for tea, it was all about The Muffin! There was much petting and playing to do, and of course fresh food and water besides her treats. When needed they even done litter box duty too. Muffin loved all of the pampering Mum and Pops gave her! Once the tea kettle began whistling, Vincent would make his way out of bed and into the kitchen. With a cup of tea at hand the four would visit until it was time for him to leave for work. Calling to him to have a good evening, Mum and Pops would then pet The Muffin some more before locking the door behind them and heading back home.

Vincent took many photos of The Muffin at his apartment on Walnut Street. Of course being The Muffin she was very photogenic! She loved posing for pictures smiling her Cat's smile.

Once a friend from England came to stay with Vincent and Muffin for a couple of days. Muffin quickly warmed up to him recognizing Matt for a lover of felines. She could always tell a true fan. Thus Muffin allowed Matt to pet her with a happy purr...

After many months of Vincent and Muffin living together at their Walnut Street apartment, Vincent became worried that The Muffin was lonely while he was at work. Since he did work at night and that was when Muffin being on Cat time was awake the most, he felt that she was by herself too much. With this thought in mind, Vincent asked Mum and Pops if they would consider bringing Muffin to live with them. Much talk was had on the subject, them hating to deprive Vincent of The Muffin. And Vincent sad to have her leave but wanting her to have as much care and attention as possible.

In the end it was decided that Muffin would come live with Mum and Pops at their place in English Village Park. Vincent would then come to visit The

Muffin, Mum and Pops, once again using his Muffin visitation rights, just as they themselves had been doing.

LIFE IN ENGLISH VILLAGE

On Muffin's moving day to Mum and Pops' place, they came to pick her up in their 1989 Toyota Corolla. Arriving at Vincent's apartment, they saw that he already had most of Muffin's packing done. The three visited and talked once more about the decision to move Muffin, still feeling it was the best thing for her. So with The Muffin riding in Mum and Pops' car and Vincent with her belongings in his car they drove to English Village Park, Vincent in his Honda and them following. Muffin being a very accomplished traveler by now done very well in the car. The only thing she did not like was overpasses. Upon arrival to their home, everyone piled out of their cars. Pops carried The Muffin while Vincent and Mum carried her things in behind him. Then with her overseeing the project, they set about arranging all of Muffin's belongings in a way that seemed to please her. Then it was all about petting her, making sure she had her food and water plus a well-attended litter box.

They all visited for a while to give Muffin and themselves time to adjust to the changes that had been made. Eventually Vincent getting up to make his leave, said he would be back again soon for Muffin visitation and of course to hang out with Mum and Pops too.

Muffin adapted to life at Mum and Pops' place in English Village Park well, her being a gypsy Cat by nature. With her keen feline intellect discovering the mysteries inside their home, she soon found the comfiest places to lie about and nap. A most important thing for a Cat to know! Having found these The Muffin roamed about sniffing, climbing and poking to inspect this newest place she called home. She found that certain tables and chairs made excellent perches for birdwatching! Muffin loved to look out the windows to watch not just birds but squirrels, rabbits and a large ground hog that had its very own name "Cocoa", for a neighbor had named him. Occasionally The Muffin came out onto the front porch to lounge on Mum and Pops' laps. Every once in a while she sniffed about in the front yard and ate some grass!

Vincent came over often to see The Muffin. She was always overjoyed to see him and enjoyed their hangout time immensely! Muffin also looked forward to all of them having a meal together. For then all three of her humans could fed her tasty tidbits! Yum. Vincent would take her photo and they would watch the ground hog do comical things.

Vincent sometimes showed them funny cat videos on his phone, Muffin couldn't believe just how stupid some of those cats were to go along with their humans. Why she thought don't they just run off or attack with tooth and claw and get away from those silly humans? Really! Cats had an image to uphold.

Every once in a while, Mum and Pops would go visit their daughter Becky and her family in Arkansas. When they took these trips, if Vincent wasn't able to come along he would do Muffin duty! Muffin thought these times were like a vacation for her. Peace and quiet with Mum and Pops gone, plus she had Vincent all to herself when he came. It was like Muffin spa time with great conversation with Vincent! He always made sure she had everything she needed. Meow! Of course she was very happy to see them when they returned. Muffin always got extra tender loving care when Mum and Pops had been away for a bit. So it was a win-win situation for The Muffin, with her receiving even more attention from all of three of her humans!

Sometimes Vincent, Mum and Pops would all go to visit Becky and her family. When this happened Muffin was treated to tiptop care. They would make sure her litter box was clean and she had lots of food and water. With tons of petting and playing with Muffin. Plus treats! Then came the part when they would drive away off on their journey to Arkansas. Muffin would watch intently from a window in the living room. Then when the car was out of sight, it was party time for The Muffin! For now she could do whatever she pleased and there was no one around to stop her. What to do first? Should she walk on top of the kitchen table and countertops? Or should she maybe sharpen her claws on something she wasn't supposed to? So many choices! Well, no matter. She would get to all of them before her humans returned that evening. What a glorious time! Muffin managed to do all of the things on her list. In between times she would stop just long enough to have something to eat and drink. She even found time to run through the house like the wild gypsy Cat that she was and kick some litter out of her litter box! By that time it was getting late in the afternoon and Muffin was beginning to wind down a bit. This she thought was the perfect time to bird watch. From the table near the window Muffin had a perfect view. She got to see lots of rabbits and squirrels too. Just about the time she was beginning to nod off into kitty Cat dreamland, The Muffin seen "Cocoa" the ground hog do some of the funniest antics she had ever seen him do. He was so very funny! Meow...Purr...Meow...Purr...

By the time Vincent, Mum and Pops made it back home in the evening, the vision that met their eyes when they opened the door was The Muffin fast asleep on top of the living room table. She opened one eye staring at us as if to say "What do you expect when you leave the Cat home alone?" Upon looking about the place, they discovered what might be cat foot prints on the kitchen table. "You think?" Plus cat hair in a few unusual areas and a fair amount of cat litter cast out of the litter box. Having made these discoveries, it was concluded that The Muffin had indeed had herself one heck of a Cat party! Not only had she eaten almost all of the food we had left her, she appeared to be completely worn out. She just laid there on the living room table as if in a Cat trance with her eyes at half-mast. Vincent, Mum and Pops just looked at each other and smiled. If Muffin was happy, they were happy! With all of them giving her a pat.

Muffin being a Cat who liked variety slept in many places in their home at English Village Park. Liking new places they never knew where they might find her sleeping. Sometimes The Muffin napped on an ottoman or one of the living room chairs. Next she could be asleep on the rug in the kitchen, or perhaps in a cardboard box in the living room. Mum and Pops would leave an empty box out just for The Muffin. Or she might be found lying in one of the kitchen chairs which also doubled as a birdwatching place should she wake up! Muffin did not however sleep in bed with them, Mum and Pops rolled around too much for her taste. A Cat just didn't know when they might get bopped and banged around! It was no way for a Cat to get her beauty rest.

Muffin loved to sit on their laps in the living room while they were reading their books. Now this was a pastime that she could really get into. Reading was a great time to snuggle and keep warm with Mum and Pops! Even though they did use her to prop their books on sometimes. She was also likely to receive lots of attention. Besides Mum and Pops' laps made awesome kitty heaters! Purr...

Muffin really liked to lie on Pops' chair ottoman next to his feet. It was her favorite place to relax when Mum and Pops watched their beloved TV show "Northern Exposure". She really liked the theme song and the quirky characters on the show. Though she could never decide what kind of animal it was that walked around a lot during the theme song. "I mean really what in the world was it?" She thought. Sometimes they tried to feed Muffin popcorn while watching "Northern Exposure". The Muffin thinking it might be a new kind of Cat treat would try to eat it. "Yuck!" She thought. "That's not a treat." So they would go and get her kitty treat snacks. "Yah! Treats and Northern Exposure with Mum and Pops." Meow...

On warm days Mum and Pops would open the front and back doors. This gave The Muffin wonderful views through the full glass storm doors that both the front and back of the home had. She would lie for hours gazing out at the birds and other wildlife. The trees, yard and porches were alive with activity. The Muffin had some excellent views of squirrels that would come on to the porches and walk on the railing. Sometimes they would walk across the porch almost to the full glass storm door. When this occurred Muffin arose and walked slowly to the glass watching intently. Then with a meow and possibly a growl she would move that squirrel along! "Who did he think he was? This was her turf."

On sunny days The Muffin would lie basking in the sun coming through the glass storm doors. It was a perfect spot to lie dreaming. On such days nothing was out of the realm of possibility. Why in such dreams a Cat could soar with all the colorful birds she seen! Or if she was hungry she could catch one to eat. Muffin sometimes even dreamed of having a huge "Tea Party" with "Cocoa" the ground hog and all of the birds, squirrels and rabbits she seen. In her dream they all sat around a massive wooden table together. Each of them was eating their favorite treats. They would communicate together in their own way. Plus Muffin would ask "Cocoa" how he accomplished some of the hilarious feats that she had seen him do! For Muffin was a fabulous dreamer of dreams...

While Muffin was living at English Village Park, Vincent, Mum and Pops came to the decision that they really needed to have Muffin's nails trimmed at the veterinary. For even while she had still lived with Vincent at his apartment on Walnut Street, she was having a terrible time with her nails getting hung up on bedspreads and rugs. Her nails were very long indeed. It seemed to make The Muffin unhappy, sometimes she even appeared embarrassed by it. So an appointment was made to have Muffin's nails trimmed. On the day of her appointment Vincent and Mum both had to work, so Pops with Muffin on his lap drove her to her nail appointment! Muffin being such a well-traveled Cat rode beautifully smiling her Cat's smile. Once there, Pops scooped her up to carry her inside the veterinary, Muffin suddenly became worried she might be moving away from her three favorite humans. Once inside she quickly understood what Pops and the Vet had in mind. The Veterinarian proceeded to trim her nails, which The Muffin vigorously disliked! Finally the vile human released her. Thankfully at that point Pops with Muffin back in his arms took her out to the car. Whew!

They drove back home with Muffin again sitting on Pops' lap which soothed her tremendously. Once they made it back home, The Muffin was fully released inside. As the remnants of the experience wore off of her, Muffin began to realize that it was much more comfortable to walk around! For her nails had become so long that they had clicked on the floor as she walked. What a relief! Now she could once again be more stealthily and sneak up on Vincent, Mum and Pops, and no more hanging up on the rugs and bedspreads either.

When Vincent and Mum arrived after work later, they all three fussed over The Muffin, observing that she was walking around with ease and seemed very happy. Noticing her three humans watching she showed them some moves she hadn't been able to do for a while! Happy to see her so carefree, they concluded that it had been very much worth the effort. High fives and Cat dances for The Muffin!

For a period of a couple of weeks Muffin slept in the music room closet, having found it left open one day after Mum and Pops had been in the room. Investigating the closet and finding it to her liking The Muffin gleefully proceeded to use the closet for napping and her all around private Cat pad! She liked it immensely. Thereafter if Mum and Pops seen Muffin walking towards the music room, they knew it was crash-pad time for The Muffin. They even had begun leaving the music room closet door ajar. That way she could hook a claw around the side of the door, opening it wide enough for her to go inside. Once Mum crept over to the music room doorway just in time to see Muffin in action opening the closet door! Mum and Pops even fixed up her newest napping spot extra cushy, so that she would be most comfortable. Sometimes when Vincent came over to visit, he upon entering would say "Where's The Muffin?"

They in turn would answer "Why don't you go check in the music room closet?" Vincent hearing this reply for the first time raised his eyebrows as if to say "What?" then went off to investigate this newest napping spot for The Muffin!

Vincent returning to the living room after his first visit to Muffin's Lair said, "She looks so darn cute in there!"

From then on Vincent knew where to look if he didn't see The Muffin. She really enjoyed it when he came to visit her in her lair! Every now and then Mum and Pops serenaded her while she lay in her comfy Cat pad in the closet. Muffin having become very musical very much enjoyed these music room jam sessions! Then after a couple of weeks Muffin once more moved on to another new napping place. This made her feel more gypsy like. But every now and then they still found her lying in her secret lair in the music room closet!

After a time in English Village Park Mum and Pops both felt the urge to move on. For they had become more gypsy like over the course of time. Also Muffin while living with them had begun to develop tummy troubles. Vincent, Mum and Pops all thought it was because she didn't get to go outdoors anymore. This was not allowed at English Village Park. So Muffin's feet hardly ever hit the ground when she was out on the porch. Knowing what a true Warrior Cat she was they wanted her to be more free. There was much to talk about it amongst Vincent, Mum and Pops, for Muffin belonged to all three of them. Therefore all decisions concerning her would be made together.

Vincent who now lived in an apartment at Polo Club wasn't sure about The Muffin living with him. For once again she would be in a place that didn't allow pets outside.

Mum and Pops after much consideration had decided to move back to St. Clair county, where they were from. They were concerned about bringing Muffin with them at least at first. They still owned eight acres in St. Clair county. But Mum and Pops would be building a home in the Walnut Grove, for there were no structures on the property. They planned to buy an RV to live in while building a cabin. So on and on the discussions went between Vincent, Mum and Pops, wondering which would be best for The Muffin. Would Vincent's apartment be best at least while they were building the cabin? Or maybe bring her along with them to live in the RV while they built it? Muffin listening to these conversations was excited knowing there was travel and some place different to live in her future! All that mattered to her was she would still have her three favorite humans.

Mum and Pops still had to put their place up for sale. They felt very optimistic in their odds of selling the place, also knowing they should have plenty of time to think about the best way to do things. Muffin for her part was just hoping to get over this confounded tummy trouble! "I mean really." she thought, "Maybe a change in locale would be the best thing for her."

The four of them became extra busy. While Vincent, Mum and Pops were at work Muffin went about Muffin duty, being the watch Cat she was responsible for security on the place. Also someone had to keep track of the comings and goings of all the wildlife milling about this place! For one never knew what those crazy squirrels or "Cocoa" the groundhog might do next. "Whew! Wore a Cat out just trying to keep track of the menagerie running around out there."

Mum and Pops having put their home up for sale in early October, found they were showing the place quite often. Muffin was always a hit with the prospective buyers who came to view their home. Everyone thought she was very charming! It seemed as though she knew what the plan was. The Muffin for her part was trying to help Mum and Pops in any way she could.

Meanwhile Mum and Pops let their workplaces know that they had put their place up for sale. Both were very understanding. Vincent came over often to talk about how everything was going. Everyone would sit in the living room and discuss possible interest in the home. Mum and Pops also talked about cabin design ideas. Plus they were all on the lookout for an RV. Vincent was impressed with Muffin for trying to help sell the place. Wow, what a Cat!

Once in October they thought they had the place sold. So were floundering about quite frantically trying to locate an RV plus storage for their belongings. The Muffin wondered if perhaps Mum and Pops had finally gone off the deep end. She became worried they might be truly going crazy. First Mum and Pops seemed happy, then they would cast about hurriedly as if they had lost something important. "I mean really it was too much for a Cat to have to deal with!" Muffin was considering enlisting Vincent's help with Mum and Pops when they finally settled down. Whew!

For Mum and Pops' part trying to sell their home at English Village Park was quite a roller coaster ride. Ending that first time with the family backing out at the last minute. As they say, try, try again. At least they weren't tearing about upsetting The Muffin! It was a bittersweet situation wanting to sell the place, but not really wanting to be so far away from Vincent.

In the midst of trying to sell their home, Mum was working at The Walnut Street Inn. It was a place she adored and also loved the people she worked with. They were all like family to her. Gary and Paula the owners/innkeepers were also trying to sell the Inn. Gary and Mum had many conversations about how both of their places would sell when they were supposed to. Wishing each other well in their next endeavors, Mum and Pops to build a cabin in St. Clair county, Gary and Paula to buy an RV and travel.

So on it went with Vincent coming over often to visit. All three of them fussed over The Muffin, who was still having tummy troubles. She loved all of the attention! Sometimes Mum and Pops had news about possible buyers of their place. Sometimes Vincent, Mum and Pops just sat and talked about travel, something all three of them loved to do. There were lots of ideas about different trips they could all go on together. Of course they would make sure The Muffin got tiptop care while we were away!

November came and with it thoughts of Thanksgiving. Muffin loved Thanksgiving, for she knew that Vincent, Mum and Pops would have a turkey. "Ah turkey" she purred. "A most lovely thing to dream of and a wonderful thing to eat!"

Mum and Pops were showing their home a couple times a week now. Interest was pretty good. Gary, the owner/innkeeper at Walnut Street Inn had a showing of the Inn long about early November. Mum and Gary were still encouraging each other and wishing the other luck.

November 7th after Mum and Pops had gone to bed, they were woke from a sound sleep by the phone ringing. The phone being on her side of the bed Mum answered it worrying about Vincent and Becky, since late night phone calls sometimes were the bearer of bad news. Muffin came walking down the hallway towards their bedroom as Mum walked out into the hall. As she answered the phone Muffin stood beside her for moral support. It was Paula. "Oh no!" saying Gary had a heart attack. Did she have Lisa the part-time Innkeeper/Manager's phone number? Mum gave her Lisa's number and then rang off.

Muffin and Mum huddled together while she next called Lisa. Answering the phone Lisa said that Gary was strong and that she felt he should be alright. Everyone would just need to jump in and help out at the Inn wherever needed. They said goodnight and Mum with a hug for The Muffin went back to bed to try and sleep.

A couple of hours later the phone rang once more. Getting out of bed Mum answered the phone as she walked up the hall towards the kitchen with Muffin meeting up with her once again. It was Lisa crying this time as she told Mum that Gary had passed away. "No!" Neither one of them could believe it. While both crying said that everyone must do their best for Paula and their daughter "Cat". Muffin, worried, stayed with her throughout all of this, while Mum pet her to comfort both of them. After their phone conversation was finished Mum hung up the phone and walked towards the bathroom to wash her face. Muffin still concerned followed along waiting in the hallway until she came out of the bathroom. As she emerged from the bathroom Muffin looked up at her as if to say "What's wrong Mum." She gave Muffin one more pat as she rubbed up against her legs. Then they both went off to try and sleep again. Both of them knowing they wouldn't.

The coming days at Walnut Street Inn were wrought with sadness. Many decisions had to be made. There were also a lot of passwords and codes that Paula, Cat and Lisa were trying to find. For Gary had been the sole user of some of these. Plus chores that Gary had always done others would needed to step in and do now. Everyone was wonderful and so giving in their efforts. All for the love of Gary, Paula and Cat. Pops and Muffin were very good to Mum when she came home from the Inn. It was very draining emotionally and physically for her. Muffin always knew Mum needed a kitty on her lap to snuggle with!

The same time that this was going on and everyone was mourning the loss of Gary; Vincent, Mum and Pops had still been looking for an RV. They found one and bought it on November 10th, which was the same day as Gary's Celebration of Life service. So after purchasing their 1984 Lance 5th wheel RV on West Sunshine Avenue, they then drove to the Inn that evening for Gary's Celebration of Life. The Inn was full of all of the employees who worked there and so were part of the Walnut Street Inn family. There were also many of Gary's family members. Plus friends and guests who had stayed at the Inn and gotten to know Gary. The Inn was filled to the brim with people who loved Gary. It was a beautiful experience. With buying the RV the same day as Gary's Celebration of Life, Mum felt like it was kind of his RV too. And that when they went up to the Walnut Grove to live in it while building their cabin, they would go in the spirit of Gary! When Mum and Pops came home later that evening there was much talk about the RV and the gathering for Gary at the Inn. The Muffin was all ears, she seemed to understand that the tide was turning and that new things were coming on all of their horizons.

The Muffin and Vincent were very excited about the RV! For even though Mum and Pops hadn't sold their home in English Village Park yet, they knew that having the RV was the first step in being ready for when it did happen. A man was hired to pull the 5th wheel RV up to the Walnut Grove in St. Clair county. He would also set it up in the spot they had chosen. Now Mum and Pops would have a place to stay while surveying the land for a good place to build their cabin and for general clearing up of tree limbs in the Walnut Grove.

Vincent, Becky and her family had lots of questions about the RV. Mum and Pops filled them in on all of the details. They were also able to show them pictures of it, even showing Muffin some of the photos of the RV. Though they weren't sure Muffin understood what Mum and Pops were trying to show her. She kept posing like she thought they were trying to take her picture. He he...

Barely over a week later Mum and Pops were contacted by a woman named Rose who very much wanted to see the home they had for sale. So November 18th she was scheduled to come have a look at it. The morning of Rose's 10am appointment Muffin scrambled about with them cleaning and tidying up the place. "Whew!" Muffin thought "I'll be ready for a nap after this human leaves." 10am came and went without Rose appearing, all began to think that she would be a no show, something that had happened a couple of times to them already. About 11:30am a truck was noticed parked out front of their place with two women in it. They were just thinking of going out to investigate when the truck drove off. The same vehicle came around again at 12:30pm but left about the time they were seen. It was finally decided that maybe they were lost. At 1pm the same truck pulled up out front again and with it also a woman in a van. This time Muffin, Mum and Pops made it to the door as all three women exited their vehicles, They discovered that it was Rose with two of her daughters. Whew! So Rose had finally made here. It seemed she had gotten side tracked because of a meeting she had with a family who wanted to buy the house she currently lived in. Yikes!

Rose and her daughters looked over the home thoroughly with Muffin, Mum and Pops in attendance in case they had any questions. It quickly became apparent that Rose upon seeing the home liked it even more. Her daughters for their part were encouraging her to buy it, saying that she wouldn't find a better deal. Wow! What? Next came the tricky part. Rose said that she wanted to buy the place but that she wouldn't have the money until December 18th, which was a month from today. That was when Rose would receive payment for the sale of her house. Mum and Pops really thought Rose was the buyer they had been looking for. Plus everyone agreed that they would need a full month to have everything sorted for an upcoming move. The hardest thing about it was without a security deposit from Rose on the home Mum and Pops would be flying by the seat of their pants! But no less than she who would be doing close to the same thing on her house.

Upon Rose and her daughters leaving that day, Muffin, Mum and Pops whooping and hollering done Cat dances in the living room. Muffin watching them flint about in a frenzy of activities, knew that they would need her on their laps in the evenings for zen Cat time. Vincent came over even more often to check on Muffin, Mum and Pops. They told Vincent all about Rose, also showing him their ever evolving cabin plans. Plus there was talk about storage options for their belongings. Becky, Abe and Ambria were told about the upcoming sale also.

Everyday became even more filled with things to do. Mum and Pops were very grateful to each have a turn with The Muffin on their laps in the evenings, for she seemed to know that they really needed a kitty on their laps! They both put in notice at their workplaces. They also found a storage facility in El Dorado Springs that would store their belongings when the time came. Right on! Mum and Pops had begun packing things that we weren't using every day too. Muffin loved all of the boxes! She was forever looking for the best one to sleep in. It was decided by Vincent, Mum and Pops that Muffin should move up to the Walnut Grove, to live in the RV with them while building the cabin. A very hard decision that was made by all three, wanting what was best for her. Thinking that country living might just be what The Muffin needed.

Thanksgiving came and with it turkey. "Yum!" thought Muffin. How she loved turkey. Mum and Pops made sure The Muffin got to have plenty, feeling she deserved it. For Muffin had been ever busy making sure Mum and Pops both had their zen Cat time in the evenings. Which was very much appreciated! Meow...

Muffin liked to hang out with Mum and Pops

while they were working on cabin designs. She really liked some of the ideas they had. Vincent also joined in when he was over, he always had many good points to make about the different cabin designs. Muffin especially liked that Vincent always kept her in mind. He would say things like "Muffin would really enjoy an upstairs. And that they should make sure that The Muffin had windows the right height for her to see out of." Ah how Muffin loved Vincent for all of his genuine Cat sense!

There were times that Muffin was very glad Mum and Pops told Vincent about their cabin ideas. One particular cabin design that Muffin became very alarmed about was the round house! Vincent had come over luckily, Mum and Pops were showing him their crazy idea about a round house. "I mean really." Muffin thought. "A round house?" It made her feel half crazy just thinking about it. She would make herself dizzy going in circles. Whew! Vincent bless him happened to mention to Mum and Pops that a round house might not be the best cabin design for Muffin. Mum and Pops upon hearing this looked over at The Muffin. Whoa they gasped! Muffin looks pretty frazzled just thinking about it. Yikes!

"Nope." Mum and Pops said. "Absolutely no round house." Muffin giving Vincent a look of loving appreciation and gratitude, breathed a huge sigh of relief. "You go Vincent!" She smiled.

So on the days went with Mum and Pops keeping in close contact with Rose. Everything seemed to be fine there. Muffin, Vincent, Mum and Pops were getting very close on the cabin design they wanted to build. The neighbor who had land adjacent to theirs in St. Clair county had been contacted. For they would need him to sign an easement release form for a pole and power line to be ran across his property, so they could have electricity. Didn't see any problem with that. Mum and Pops then made a journey up to the Walnut Grove, wanting to study the property and decide on the best building spot. Plus ready the RV for when Muffin and they would be moving in.

December came quickly it seemed. With it more packing of belongings. Muffin really enjoyed the boxes. "Which one to sleep in today?" she wondered. Muffin, Vincent, Mum and Pops all knew that Christmas would be different this year. December 18th was still the home sale and moving date. All of them had decided that they would just have to figure it out after the move. Knowing a good time would be had no matter where Christmas was spent.

Now it was getting down to the wire! The Muffin, Mum and Pops had reserved a U-Haul truck. Planning to pick it up two days before the moving date, Pops had finished up at his workplace in the first part of December. With December 18th only seven days away now, Mums last day at The Walnut Street Inn on the other hand was on a Tuesday. The same day slotted to pick up the U-Haul, and only two days before their home sale and moving date.

Driving away from The Walnut Street Inn on her last day, Mum and Pops were on the way to pick up the U-Haul when everything suddenly seemed very clear and yet out of focus at the same time. Upon arriving back to English Village Park that day, they managed to get the U-Haul backed up and parked, parking the Jeep beside it. Then upon opening the door to go inside, that's when things really started to get out of kilter! Muffin was giving them the look like "What the hell is that big thing in our driveway?"

In that moment Muffin, Mum and Pops realized just how much they would have to do to be ready to move in two days! Vincent was working both days and would be unable to help with the packing and loading up. It was up to the three of them to make this thing happen. It was a good thing they were an above average team! "Teamwork." Mum and Pops chanted to The Muffin. She gave them a knowing look as if to say "We've got this." So after snacks and drinks for all, they began the major task of packing and loading the U-Haul.

They steadily packed and loaded their belongings into the U-Haul, from early afternoon until after dark that Tuesday evening. They stopped only to eat a quick bite and pow wow with The Muffin. All three of them were tired but couldn't get their brains to shut off. Tomorrow morning the three of them would get up extra early so that they could be in El Dorado Springs to unload the U-Haul about 7am. After this decision was made The Muffin, Mum and Pops all lay down on a frameless mattress on the living room floor, to try to get some rest. Purr...zzz...

Wednesday morning came quickly. The Muffin with eyes only at half-mast walked them to the door. Having fed, watered and petted her up, Mum and Pops told The Muffin to hold down the fort. As they drove off in the U-Haul, a yawning Muffin went back to bed hoping to get a little more rest in while they were gone doing this unloading business. Thank goodness she couldn't be expected to help with such a thing! Arriving in El Dorado Springs, Mum and Pops drove to their storage unit. Carefully they began unloading belongings into the storage unit trying to make the most of the area. It was a daunting task.

Finished unloading they stopped just long enough to get take-out from McDonald's. Then began the trip back, eating as they drove while planning ahead for the next load of belongings, both of them were ready to go hangout with The Muffin!

By the time Mum and Pops made it back to English Village Park, they knew they were really going to have to step it up a notch. It was around 2pm and Muffin met them at the door. Happy to see her, they gave her a good petting! They also made sure she had plenty of food and water while drinking their caffeine. Then it was back to packing and reloading the U-Haul. Having talked to Rose earlier while on the road, 1pm tomorrow December 18th they would be meeting her at her bank. Whew! There was still a ways to go before then.

By 8pm that Wednesday evening all three of them realized they were in trouble! There was still loading to be done, so after having a meeting to talk things over, Mum and Pops proceeded to pour themselves special drinks called "Muffin Cups" just for loading. Then turning on some music as well with Muffin to supervise they set to work. Mum on the inside of the home and Pops on the shop/storage shed out back. Working like moles in the dark outside loading the U-Haul since there wasn't hardily any light to be had, they stopped only to replenish their special drinks now and then and pet The Muffin. With some cursing involved and hoping that the neighbors would let them slide for working so late, a little after 11pm they finally finished loading the U-Haul. The only thing left to load being the mattress mostly. Exhausted they all lay down at midnight to get a few hours sleep.

At 3am in the morning Muffin, Mum and Pops stumbled out of bed. Blurry-eyed the three went about dressing and having something to eat and drink. Then biding Muffin goodbye and that they would be back soon, drove the U-Haul out of English Village Park. This was the Day, Thursday December 18th, it was time to make things happen today! Driving once again to El Dorado Springs, Mum and Pops unloaded the U-

Haul. They were very thankful the storage unit had a light inside, since it was totally dark being only 6am on this winter morning. Unloading belongings into the storage unit they hoped that it was big enough. Whew! It was going to be close. But as luck would have it there was just enough room. Yah!

Climbing back into the U-Haul, they drove on back. The U-Haul had to be returned by 11am. Stopping long enough to get gas and a breakfast sandwich besides some caffeine, Mum and Pops headed back to English Village Park, so Mum could follow Pops in the Jeep back to the U-Haul rental place. Making it there around 10:30am, the U-Haul got checked back in and then off they went to see how The Muffin was. The only things left in our place now was Muffin, her belongings and a box she seemed to like. She met them at the door with a look that clearly said "What on earth did you do with all of the furniture?" So they fussed over her for a while. Making sure Muffin's food, water and litter box were well attended to.

It was getting close to noon by this time, so telling The Muffin they would be back soon, the two of them drove off in the Jeep to find a place to eat, before meeting Rose at her bank. After a meal they began looking for Rose's bank. After a bit of driving they found what appeared to be her bank and parking the Jeep sat inside it to wait. They were early but 15 minutes passed without Rose appearing, Pops called her daughters phone number and after talking to her, he got off the phone saying they were at the wrong branch of her bank!

So starting the Jeep they drove to where Rose was supposed to be. Pulling into the parking lot they looked for her van and also went inside the bank looking for her. Still no Rose. They waited around awhile, then with heavy hearts drove back to their home. As they came inside Muffin could see that Mum and Pops were upset. She rubbed up against their legs hoping to make them feel better. But Mum and Pops were pretty freaked out! "What was going on? Had Rose never really aimed to buy their home? What were they going to do now? Most of their belongings were in a storage unit in El Dorado Springs for pete sakes! Muffin, her kitty stuff and a very small amount of their belongings were all they had. Just enough for living in an RV. "I mean what the hell!" Pops had been calling Rose, but Rose wasn't answering her phone. The Muffin watching was beginning to really worry about Mum and Pops. She kept rubbing against their legs trying to comfort them. "Meow?" She ask. Maybe they needed some Warrior Cat help!

Suddenly the phone started ringing! Pops grabbing it answered "Hello?" It was Rose! Yikes. She was crying saying she still wanted to buy their home, but the bank had told her she would have to wait 24 hours for the cashiers check to clear from the sale of her house. Whoa! Could she come meet us at our place tomorrow? Rose said she would have the money with her to buy their place when she came. Looking around, Pops thought "Do we have a choice?" He replied "Alright Rose. What time will you be here?"

She said "Is noon alright?"

And he said "O.k." After Pops got off the phone with Rose. He ask Mum, "Did you get most of that?"

She replied looking around the bare interior of their home and then at Muffin and Pops, "Do you think Rose will really show up with the money?"

Pops looking at The Muffin and Mum said "We're going to have to hope so. What else can we do?" So it was decided after the three of them talked it over, that they would be driving up in the Jeep to their RV. They would spend the night there. Then Mum and Pops would come back tomorrow and met with Rose. "Sure hope she comes this time." Whew...

Muffin listening to Mum and Pops talk thought, "Sounds like it's about time for us to hit the road!" Oh how she loved riding in a vehicle!

After Pops had loaded all of Muffin's belongings into the Jeep, Mum got into the passenger side. Pops carried The Muffin out and putting her on Mum's lap, shut the door. Getting in the driver's side Pops said "Let get this show on the road!"

Muffin excitedly listening meowed "This gypsy Cat is ready. Let's go!" Mum put on some travel tunes as the three of them rolled out of English Village Park and up the road toward St. Clair county!

OUR TINY RV HOME

A s Pops drove along Muffin sitting on Mum's lap
looked out the window at the changing scenery
as they left the city behind. She was enjoying
riding in the Jeep immensely! As the landscape
changed to trees, fields and pastures, Muffin noticing
some sort of beast in the pastures wondered what
those animals could be. Mum noticing the direction of
her gaze exclaimed to Pops, "Wow! I bet this is the
first time Muffin has ever seen cows." Her ears perked
at this new discovery of what these beast were. The
farther north they went the more cows Muffin saw.

Muffin began to wonder where all of the humans
had gone. She had never seen so few of them before.
Had the cows perhaps ran the humans off? Would
there be cows near the RV where Mum, Pops and her
would be living? If so perhaps she could spy on the
cows from afar and learn more about them. She sure
hoped they were friendly!

After Mum and Pops had stopped at a brightly lit

place called The Pilot, they sang out, "We're almost home now!" 30 minutes later Pops turned onto a gravel road off of the highway.

Muffin feeling a little rattled wondered "What on earth happened to the highway?" She had never been on a gravel road before. "Yikes!" She shuddered.

Mum and Pops noticing The Muffin's distress said, "It's alright Muffin we're almost there!" While petting her to soothe her.

Pops turned onto yet another gravel road. Muffin looking out the side window saw many cows in the pastures and more trees too. Suddenly he turned into a Walnut Grove surrounded by pastures that had cows in them. Mum called out, "We're here!"

Muffin looking around seen the RV just as they drove passed a beautiful tall Cedar tree. "Whoa!" She thought, "We do have cows for neighbors." Already looking forward to studying them to learn their ways.

As Mum and Pops pulled the Jeep up in front of the RV, they sang out, "Come on Muffin let's go see our tiny RV home!"

Muffin looking up at the sky realized everything seemed bigger out here in the country. "Wow! Look at all that space." She marveled. Pops coming around to the passenger side of the Jeep scooped her up and carried her towards the RV.

Opening the RV door Mum said "We finally made it Muffin. Let's get you settled in."

Climbing up into the RV with her in his arms Pops said, "Welcome to our little RV, Home sweet home!"

Muffin looking around mused, "This really is a tiny home." Pops put her down in the sitting area around a small round table. Then Mum and him went back out to the Jeep to bring in all of their belongings. Looking out the windows that surrounded the table she noticed that she could see the cows perfectly from here. She also realized it was getting dark. "Whoa!" Muffin wondered why Mum and Pops didn't turn on the lights. It was getting hard to see inside the RV. That's when she heard Mum and Pops say there wasn't any electricity yet and also that they would need to go somewhere down the road to Mum's ole home place to get water, because we didn't have running water here either. So after they turned on some battery powered lighting, Pops drove down to the ole home place to get some water. Mum stayed behind to finish setting the place up and keep The Muffin company.

Mum began getting their tiny RV home in ship shape as she started supper, while Muffin prowled around the place inspecting it. She checked out the tiny bathroom, and all the low to the floor storage doors and drawers. Then climbing up into the bedroom alcove Muffin checked the comfy blankets and pillows, kneading them a bit. Then looking around she noticed happily all of the windows surrounding the bed. Just as she saw lights coming down the lane towards the RV, suddenly realizing it was Pops, Muffin watched as he got out of the Jeep carrying jugs towards the RV. Mum opening the door took the jugs from him saying it sure was good to have water. "Yay!" Muffin purred, "Mum and Pops were smart. They knew how to have lights and water without really having lights and water." She also discovered the RV had just the right height of a heater. It was like her own private kitty heater!

Mum and Pops called to her saying, "Suppertime Muffin!"

"Supper!" Smiling her Cat's smile, "Yahoo!" Muffin jumped down out of bedroom alcove with only a tiny bit of difficulty because of it being such a small space. She padded the few steps over to where they

were near the table. Mum and Pops showed Muffin all
of her amenities. Food check, water check, treats
check and her litter box. "Meow!" She smiled. Mum
and Pops always made sure she had everything she
needed. Fixing their plates they sat down in the
seating alcove around the table, with Muffin's food
bowls beside them on the floor. They enjoyed their
first meal in the tiny RV home together. The lighting
was very dim being battery powered, so Mum and
Pops couldn't see very well. Muffin of course having
Cat eyes could see perfectly.

After they had cleared up the supper dishes, Mum
said, "I think it's time to get comfy." That's when
Muffin, Mum and Pops came to the conclusion that
only one of them at a time could do anything major in
their tiny space. Everything required absolute
cooperation. If someone wanted to change clothes
they would say, "I'm going to change clothes now,"
with the others finding a seat out of the way. After
Mum and Pops had got comfy, they gathered cups,
toothbrushes, water and toothpaste to brush their
teeth outside. Their bathroom duties were done
outside too.

"Mmm" Muffin mused, "So that's what it means
for humans if they don't have indoor plumbing." She
observed as Mum came back in and used some sort of
disposable cloth on her face to clean up with. Pops
coming back inside poured Mum and himself water
out of a jugs into cups for both of them. He even
topped off Muffin's water bowl. She was very
impressed. Mum and Pops knew lots of new tricks.
When they had lived in the city she had worried that
Mum and Pops were becoming too set in their ways.
The Muffin was happy to see that wasn't the case. This
was starting to look more and more like a real
dventure for all of them. Yeah!

Once the three of them had settled in around the table in the tiny alcove, Pops saying he was ready for something a little stronger than water, stood up to retrieve their special drink supplies from inside the sink cabinet. Mum sang out, "Me too!" Sitting back down Pops poured their special drink aka "Muffin Cups" into their coffee cups. Which would become their all around cup for drinking everything.

"Whew!" Muffin sighed, "These last 48 hours have been wild! Even for this wild gypsy Cat." They sat in the tiny alcove enjoying each others company in the dim light. Muffin lay between Mum and Pops on a fuzzy blanket that they had brought along so she would be extra comfy. While petting The Muffin they talked, she listened feeling rather drowsy.

As Muffin listened to their conversation she heard Mum ask, "Well do you think Rose will show up with the money to buy our home tomorrow?"

Pops looking a little less than totally confident replied, "But surely she will, Rose has to have a place to live too. She just sold her house!"

Mum sighed, "I hope you're right! I don't like to think of what we might have to do if she doesn't come through with the money." Upon hearing this Muffin sat up a little straighter deciding she had better pay more attention to their conversation. Wondering what they meant by that. She heard Mum and Pops say they would be driving back to English Village Park tomorrow. They were to meet Rose there at noon for the sale of their home. Considering that Mum and Pops had been turning other possible buyers of their place away, saying that they had a buyer for it already, they sure hoped so. They told Muffin that she could stay home in the RV which would give her some time to birdwatch and start on her study of the cows.

"That would be fun!" She thought, "But when will

you be back?" This place was new to her yet.

Mum and Pops watching The Muffin realized she was a little worried they might not come back. "Oh it's alright Muffin." Mum soothed, "We will be back right after the sale goes through tomorrow. Probably 3 or 4 in the afternoon."

Muffin breathed a huge sigh of relief. "Thank goodness!" She sighed, "Mum and Pops are coming back then. Good!"

The three of them stayed up late that first night in the RV. There was much talk about the things they would need to make the place more homey. Like a wash pan for dishes, a small bowl to fit in the tiny RV bathroom sink and a bucket to fit in the toilet for night use in cold weather. That way they would be able to wash dishes and use the tiny bathroom for some of Mum and Pops' cleanup. Muffin lying between them once more relaxed now that she was no longer worried about being left alone to live with the cows, marveled at some of Mum and Pops' creative ideas for this temporary alternative lifestyle they would all be living. Only until they got electricity, got their cabin built, and had a well drilled they told Muffin. Pops would text their neighbor about the easement tomorrow while Mum drove them to English Village Park to meet Rose. Mum said, "Just think Muffin, you'll be able to explore the RV all you want and nap whenever you feel like it while we're gone tomorrow!"

Muffin upon hearing this thought, "Well when you put it like that, Heck yah! I'm going to have me a time while Mum and Pops are away! Meow!"

At this point with midnight approaching and all of them yawning profusely, Pops stated that he thought it time they turned in for the night. Mum with another huge yawn said, "Yes I think so." After going outside for bathroom duty, they came back inside saying, "Come on Muffin it's bedtime!" Muffin hearing this jumped down from the seating alcove. Padding over to her food and water, she had a nibble and a drink of water. Then she stepped into her litter box a moment. Mum and Pops setting an alarm for in the morning, both climbed into the bedroom alcove. They had just got settled under the blankets, when The Muffin jumping up onto the bed lay down between Mum and Pops kneading and purring until she was quite comfortable. "Ahh." Muffin sighed sleepily.

Pops suddenly exclaimed, "Look at all those stars and that moon! Isn't it great having all of these windows in our bedroom alcove?"

Muffin almost asleep purred, "It sure is Pops!" Even though all of them knew that tomorrow would have an uncertain outcome, Muffin, Mum and Pops slept well under a moon and starlit sky. Sleeping the sleep of the physically and emotionally exhausted. Zzzzzz...

The alarm went off before first light the next morning. Mum and then Pops stumbled out of bed doing their best to get dressed and comb their hair in the dim light of the RV. Muffin with her eyes only half open jumped down from the bedroom alcove. Pops stepped outside for bathroom duty, while Mum pet Muffin then freshened up her food and water bowls. As he came back in, Mum took her turn outside. Pops put the kettle on the gas stove to heat water. When the kettle whistled they fixed their hot drinks before sitting down with Muffin in the tiny seating alcove. None of them were very awake and mostly they just looked around the RV in the dim battery powered light and gazed out of the windows at the approaching dawn. Pops breaking the silence said, "Sure is a lot quieter here than in English Village Park." Muffin and Mum looked over at Pops nodding their agreement not wishing to break the silence yet. Dawn was fast approaching and with it full daylight. It seemed best shared between them without words.

Daylight seemed to break the spell. They began to talk quietly about the coming day and also what to do about breakfast. Now that they were able to see better in the RV, Mum standing up said she was going to put on her makeup and fix her hair. When finished she said, "Alright what shall we have for breakfast!" It was decided that Mum and Pops would have a snack breakfast and then stop at The Pilot for a breakfast sandwich on the way to English Village Park. Muffin's bowls were refilled and treats were given much to her delight!

Starting the Jeep so it could warm up a bit, they gave a last snuggle and pat to The Muffin saying. "Have fun bird and cow watching! We will be back this afternoon."

Muffin watching Mum and Pops drive up the lane and then off down the gravel road thought, "Oh boy! Now I can really explore the RV and study the birds and cows!" There hadn't been much time to do that yesterday since they had arrived at their tiny RV home late in the afternoon. She sure hoped Mum and Pops' meeting with Rose went well. Whew!

So all of that day was very quiet except for the sounds that Muffin made while prowling around and jumping up into the bedroom alcove. She had decided to work on her ascend and descend from the bed. When satisfied that she had improved greatly, Muffin stopping long enough for a snack and a litter box break, got on top of the table in the seating alcove. She was beginning to realize that country living was so quiet she could hear the birds twittering and hear the cows walking in the pasture outside. Not only that but she was able to watch the cows when they went back home. After enjoying these activities for quite some time, she hopped down from her perch on the table. Kneading her blanket in the seating alcove Muffin settled down upon it for a good Catnap! Purr... Later upon waking Muffin had a lovely midday meal. Then she poked about pawing at all the low doors and drawers to see if any of them opened easily. A couple of them did. Meow! Fun exploring for The Muffin. Once the maximum amount of poking about had been done, she was off to try jumping up into the bedroom alcove. Ready. Set. Big jump. Yes! She aced it. Cat dances for The Muffin! Wow! Pops was right having all of these windows in the bedroom alcove was awesome. From this side of the RV Muffin had a good view of that magnificent Cedar tree and the pretty lane going up to the gravel road. As she watched a car came up the road. "Whoa! Is that Mum and Pops? No." Muffin mused, "That's not our red Jeep." She thought that according to the light that they should be back in 2 to 3 hours. Suddenly something caught Muffin's eye. Over near the big Cedar tree were 2 red squirrels running about. She enjoyed the squirrels antics for quite awhile. They were very entertaining! After the squirrels went off to wherever squirrels go, Muffin lounged about on the bed birdwatching in between naps.

She had been snoozing for quite some time, dreaming of yummy cat treats and all of the petting she would get when Mum and Pops got back. When all at once Muffin woke with a start, realizing she was hearing something. Looking up the lane towards the big Cedar tree, the red Jeep suddenly appeared with Mum and Pops in it. "Wow." She marveled, "That was some powerful dream!"

Parking the Jeep near the RV they carried shopping bags inside seeming in good spirits. Muffin standing on the ledge of the bedroom alcove welcomed them home. "Hi Muffin!" they chimed shutting the RV door behind them. Then saying. "Rose came and bought our home! Just like she said she would. Yahoo! We did it Muffin."

"Meow! If Mum and Pops were happy she was happy too," purred The Muffin.

Smiling they said, "Tonight we celebrate!" Muffin smiled her agreement. Watching intently as they unpacked their shopping bags, she saw that Mum and Pops had indeed bought for their tiny RV home a wash pan, a small bowl for the tiny RV sink and also a pail for the RV toilet.

Then out of another shopping bag came what she had been waiting for, yummy treats and cat food. "Cat dances for The Muffin!" "Yah!" She purred, Mum and Pops had remembered she was out of treats. It looked like they had gotten treats for themselves as well.

"Tonight we feast and make merry!" said Pops. So they set about putting away any food or drink items that wouldn't be needed for their house party. Mum and Pops also installed the wash pan, small bowl and pail where they were needed. Happily going about these tasks with The Muffin supervising. Finished readying the place for their house party, they suddenly realized it was almost twilight. Mum turning on some of the battery powered lights said, "Looks like we better clean up and get ourselves ready before it gets totally dark." Just as they had when putting away their shopping, Muffin, Mum and Pops fell into their dance of taking turns getting ready for the night in their tiny space.

Freshened up and comfy for their party. They settled in around the tiny table to enjoy their treats.

"Yummy!" they all said as one. Sitting in the dim lighting around the table, they were able to really focus on each other's company. The dim lights seemed to cut out all the distractions, making Muffin, Mum and Pops feel as if they could see one another more clearly, even though the light was very faint or maybe because of it. Each of them instinctively knew that this tiny RV home with its dim lighting and rural setting was going to bring them closer together than they had ever been before. This new found connectedness made for an even more lively super-charged celebration. Mum and Pops raised their "Muffin Cups" in salute as they clinked their cups together while Muffin sighed happily. Eventually settling into bed around midnight again later that night. They fell asleep while gazing up at the stars, snuggled together in their bedroom alcove.

Waking the next morning before daylight they went about their morning toilette in the faint light. After fixing their cups of joe, Mum and Pops sat down at the table with Muffin to plan their first day living in the Walnut Grove. Pops was having trouble reaching their neighbor about signing the land easement papers to run electricity to their property. Hopefully Mum and Pops could meet with him soon. Although with Christmas only five days away, things might take a little longer. Also they could go ahead with pricing building materials while waiting to get electricity to their property. Electricity would run the power tools necessary to help build their cabin.

Meanwhile Christmas plans were finalized with Becky and Vincent on the phone. The holiday celebrations would be at Becky's this year it was decided. Mum and Pops would also go to his Mom and Louis' house to visit around Christmastime too. Muffin was looking forward to having a Cat party in their tiny RV home while her humans were away. Meow!

That sunny December day, Muffin, Mum and Pops went outside to begin clearing off the old house foundation. Mum told Muffin that there used to be an old barn-style house on the foundation. She also said they were thinking of building their cabin or workshop on top of it. "Wow! If other humans had once lived here, then other cats had probably lived there too," The Muffin mused. She was thoroughly enjoying being outside. While Mum and Pops raked and pruned the old house foundation, she investigated the foundation. So many sights and sounds that was new to her. Looking up at birds in the trees, Muffin just couldn't believe how big the sky was out here in the country! It had never seemed so large to her while she lived in the city. The air was even different here. Fresher!

Muffin noticing some tin lying on the ground near the old house foundation walked over to see it more closely. She was just about to get a look up under the tin when Mum said. "No no, Muffin. There's an old well underneath that tin."

"Rats! What's an old well?" She wondered. It made her even more curious. But they would not let her go near it and secured the tin on top of the well more firmly with large pieces of wood. Muffin guessed for now that she would just have to leave it alone. Besides Mum and Pops were talking of starting a fire on top of the foundation to burn it off. "Yikes!" She thought. "A fire? This cat can do without that! What about her beautiful fur for pete sakes?"

Just then Pops remarked. "I don't think Muffin's going to like being out here when we start the fire."

Muffin eyeing them both thought, "You got that right Pops!"

Mum scooping her up said. "Come on Muffin I'll bet you'd like to go hang out in the RV."

The Muffin with a huge sigh looked up at Mum thinking, "You're darned right I want to go to the RV!"

As Mum brought her inside the RV, she freshened up Muffin's bowls and gave her some treats. "Now you can relax." Mum said, "We'll be back in just a little while."

Long about dinnertime Mum came back inside to check on Muffin and fix something to eat. She had a distinct smoky smell about her but at least Muffin could see that the fire was mostly out, thankfully. She could see Pops walking around the old foundation checking to make sure. Every once and awhile he used a shovel to pound on a spot that was lightly smoking. Satisfied, Pops walked to the RV. Coming in he told them, "The fire is all out and the foundation burnt off really well."

"Whew." sighed Muffin. "What a relief!" Then they gathered around the table for their midday meal. Mum and Pops had decided to go to town and check lumber prices this afternoon. Telling Muffin that they would pick up a few supplies while they were at it, then get some water on the way back. Feeling a bit tired after her meal She purred, "Quiet time for The Muffin!"

Mum and Pops were gone for several hours that afternoon, which gave Muffin plenty of time to get a good nap in before she watched the birds and squirrels at play. Then it was all about studying those cows. Having never seen a cow before Muffin found them fascinating. All together a very pleasant afternoon! Coming back later Mum and Pops talked about lumber prices and the gifts they had picked up for Christmas with the family. They sat down with The Muffin and gave her a good petting. Afterwards they went through the bags of Christmas gifts and holiday treats, letting Muffin play with the empty bags much to her delight. She especially enjoyed it when Mum and Pops let the bags just float to the floor. Meow!

After supper that evening Mum and Pops talked of putting a price list together for the cabin. They planned to write it out on paper tomorrow with the prices they had gotten from the local lumberyard. It was too dim to do so this evening.

Muffin lying between Mum and Pops on her blanket enjoyed listening to their conversation while they each petted her in turn. There was so much excitement in the air about the cabin and the land they were going to build it on. The three of them were going to live free from the everyday rat race. Here in their Walnut Grove they were going to build the life that they wanted. Muffin listening thought, "You've got that right. Let's live like wild Cats!" Laying down to sleep that night they dreamed of their cabin in the Walnut Grove. zzz...

Rolling out of bed early the next morning. Muffin, Mum and Pops fell into their dance in and around each other as they got dressed and completed their toilette. Coming back inside from their outdoor bathroom excursion, Mum and Pops turned off the whistling kettle and fixed steaming cups of caffeine. Freshening up Muffin's bowls they sat down at the table to have their first cup of joe. Talking quietly as they watched the eastern sky slowly get light. It brightened the dim interior of their tiny RV home with its soft glow.

With daylight upon them, they went about fixing breakfast. Then sitting down to eat Mum and Pops gave Muffin tasty tidbits they thought she might like. Finding the ham to her liking she nibbled on it. Hash browns on the other hand were not Muffin food.

"What exactly were hash browns anyway?" She wondered, "They just didn't taste right." After clearing away the breakfast dishes Mum and Pops got out paper and pen to begin running figures on the cabin cost. They had decided upon a very basic cabin, one that would be fairly easy to build and could always be added onto later if need be.

Muffin lying on her blanket in the seating alcove listened as Mum and Pops went about figuring out how much lumber and other materials they would need to begin building their cabin. "Wow!" Muffin thought. "That sounds like a lot." She had never seen a house built before, so she didn't understand everything they talked about. But Mum and Pops seemed to so Muffin wasn't worried. It was all very exciting!

Around 11am Mum and Pops were taking a break from figuring when they heard a pickup coming down the lane. As a man and woman got out of the pickup, Muffin wondered who they might be. "Oh! It was Mum's sister Sue with her husband Ross." They had come to visit and check out the RV. "Yah!" purred Muffin, "Their first company." It was good to get to meet some of Mum's family. Muffin hoped they would see Vincent sometime soon too!

Later as they were leaving Sue and Ross said, "Let us know if you need anything." as they drove off up the lane. Smiling Muffin, Mum and Pops went back inside their tiny RV home to fix some dinner.

Afterwards they had just stepped outside to get a breath of fresh air, when they heard something coming across the pasture from the west. Muffin, Mum and Pops saw an ATV coming in their direction. It looked like their neighbor Colby was checking his cattle. Walking on over closer to talk to him they asked when a good time would be for him to meet with them and sign easement papers. It was then that Mum and Pops began to realize that Colby did not intend to sign the easement papers, he thought it would devalue his land. They told Colby that Mums' brother Scott and wife Melonie had already signed easement papers. They didn't seem concerned about their land value. Mum and Pops were very thankful they had done this for them. They asked Colby to just think about it. Muffin hearing this conversation thought it appeared that the cows might have more sense than their owner. Made her want to give him the tooth and the claw! Grrr...

Needless to say Muffin, Mum and Pops were thrown into a bit of a tailspin after their conversation with Colby. There was really no other options for running electricity to their property. Since all the other ways were at least twice as expensive. They had a budget to work with and going across Colby's land was the best and most budget friendly way. He had given them no indication of when or if he would let them know a decision. They could only hope that it would be soon. Deciding they had thought enough about the topic of electricity for now, Muffin, Mum and Pops went about the next few days working around the place. They put in a mailbox and there was a couple of lightning struck trees that needed cut. They called and talked to Becky and Vincent too. Muffin really enjoyed it when Mum put the phone up to her ear so that Vincent could talk to her. She sure missed him. Mum and Pops said that he would be coming up to visit soon. "Yah for Vincent!" She purred. Pops also called his mom and talked to her for a while. Muffin watched as he walked up and down the lane while on the phone with her.

Christmas Eve came and that evening the three of them had a festive snack feast in their tiny RV home.

Muffin enjoyed the tasty tidbits Mum and Pops shared with her. Theirs was a very casual and merry feast! For they had come to really appreciate their time together in the dim light around the table. In this adventure here in the Walnut Grove, they were together all for one and one for all!

Christmas morning they awoke early. Before getting out of bed Mum and Pops sang out, "Merry Christmas Muffin! Merry Christmas to us all!" Smiling they got out of bed and began their dance to get dressed, put the kettle on and do their toilette rituals.

Mum giving The Muffin a snuggle reached into a cabinet saying, "Look Muffin we bought you a gift!"

Her eyes opening a little wider she wondered, "What? What is it Mum?"

"Pops and I got you a new flavor of treats and a catnip mouse," she said.

"Meow!" purred Muffin as she rubbed against their legs. Pops filled her bowls then gave her some of the new treats. While Muffin enjoyed her Christmas treats, Mum and Pops sipped their hot drinks and had a small bite to eat. Giving Muffin a pat they tossed her the catnip mouse to play with. Upon smelling the catnip mouse she went wild wallowing it and batting it about. "This smells wonderful!" Meowed The Muffin, "What a wonderful Christmas gift!"

Mum and Pops were traveling to Arkansas today. They were driving to Vincent's apartment and then riding with him to Becky's place. So after Christmas breakfast and Muffin's catnip mouse playing time, they loaded the Jeep while it warmed up for their trip. Then giving The Muffin a good snuggle they sang out, "Have fun with your catnip mouse! We'll be back this evening."

As they drove off down the gravel road, Muffin looking around noticed they had topped off her bowls and even left out some more of those new yummy treats." Mum and Pops were the best!" purred The Muffin as she went off to play with the catnip mouse. By noontime, Muffin was worn out from playing with the mouse, plus all the bird, squirrel and cow watching. "Whew!" She mused, "That was some morning." Walking over to the feast Mum and Pops had left for her, Muffin had herself one heck of a Christmas dinner. Jumping up into the seating alcove afterwards she lay down upon her fuzzy blanket for a good nap. ZZZ...purr...ZZZ...purr...

Waking up several hours later Muffin drowsed for awhile. Then rousting herself jumped down to have a snack and visit the litter box. Feeling more fully awake afterwards, she climbed up into the bedroom alcove to sight see out of the windows up there. Looking about, Muffin saw some sort of animals with springy feet jump the wire fence that surrounded the Walnut Grove. "Whoa!" Muffin wondered, "What are those things? They sure can jump!" She watched as these animals roamed about in the Walnut Grove. "At least they seem friendly." She mused. As she watched the strange animals stopped eating grass and their little white tails started flipping up and down. Then suddenly these beasts bolted toward another fence, jumping over it with no effort whatsoever. The springy footed beasts then ran with such speed that they were out of sight in no time at all. "Outstanding!" Muffin enthused. She had always admired speed and agility. If only she knew what kind of beast they were. She hoped to see more of them soon.

By then it was almost dark inside the RV. Not a problem for The Muffin who had cat eyes. "Now," she thought, it's time to look at the stars!" Muffin had never seen stars so bright as they were here in the Walnut Grove. She had been star gazing for maybe half an hour, when she saw lights coming up the gravel road. As she watched they turned in at their lane. Then the Jeep with Mum and Pops in it was parking in front of the RV. "Yah! They're home!" Muffin purred.

Mum and Pops carrying a few odds and ends with them came inside the RV. Turning on their battery powered lights they sang out, "Hi Muffin! Did you have a fun day?"

Muffin reviewing the day thought, "I sure did!"

Seeing that she was content Mum replied, "That's good. We had fun too."

Pops remarked, "That it was good to see Vincent, Becky and her family." They both washed up and got comfortable, afterwards sitting down with some snacks and drinks. They had all come to love this ritual of hanging out together around their table. It being Christmas made it even more special. Lying on her blanket between them, Muffin was just starting to become sleepy-eyed when Pops exclaimed, "Boy that sure was a lot of deer tracks we seen driving down the lane this evening! Did deer come and visit you Muffin?"

Sitting up a little taller she looked at Pops. "Is that what they were? Deer? Yes they sure did come and visit me!" She smiled.

Mum noticing her surprised look exclaimed, "Why I bet that was Muffin's first time seeing deer."

Muffin staring sleepy-eyed at them mused, "Ah another mystery solved!" Turning into bed that night the three of them gazed at the moon and stars. The moon was so bright that the Walnut trees cast shadows onto the ground. It was magical. "What a wonderful Christmas!" Muffin sighed as she drifted off to sleep.

The following morning they arose early. After

Muffin, Mum and Pops performed their morning rituals, they sat around the table to enjoy their first cup of joe. Muffin more awake now that she had eaten her breakfast thought, "Oh yeah Mum and Pops are going to visit his Mom and Step-Dad today."

So after breakfast Mum and Pops started the Jeep up and then loaded what they were bringing with them. After checking Muffin's food bowls they gave her some of those new treats she liked so well. The Muffin was given much petting while they waited for the Jeep to warm up. It was a bit nippy out this morning so they had donned their winter clothing. Muffin looking at them all bundled up thought, "It sure is a shame Mum and Pops don't have a fur coat to keep them warm like I do. He he."

Ready to go now Pops said, "Hold down the fort while we're away Muffin. Hope you see some more deer today!" Saying they would return late this afternoon Mum and Pops headed off down the gravel road and out of sight.

It was just now beginning to get light in the east. For they had left very early. Muffin still feeling kind of tired decided to climb up into the bedroom alcove. She had a great view up there from three directions. "Good." Yawned Muffin. "This way I can sight see in between cat naps!" So she dozed for a while having dreams about the deer she had seen yesterday. Waking up midmorning Muffin climbing down from the bedroom alcove decided to see if she could find any low doors or drawers that she might be able to open. After much pawing about she got one door open! Looking inside she discovered that was where Mum and Pops kept her litter box tools. Pawing it back shut Muffin thought, "I could use a litter box break and then a snack sounds good." It had turned into a lovely sunny day. So after her snack Muffin jumped up onto the table where she had a great view of the cows. She studied them for quite awhile. Then decided to hop down onto her blanket in the seating alcove to give herself a good bath. Feeling ever so clean afterwards, she paid a visit to her bowls and had a nice meal. "This feels a like a spa day!" purred The Muffin.

By the time Muffin seen Mum and Pops coming up the gravel road in the late afternoon, she'd had a totally zen day and was looking forward to spending the evening with them. As Mum and Pops parked the Jeep in front of their tiny RV home, Muffin waited expectantly by the door for them to come inside. Pops opening the door said, "Hi Muffin! Would you like to come outside and get some fresh air?"

With no hesitation she bound out the door. "There was so much to see." mused The Muffin. And her nose could never get quite enough of all this fresh air! Mum and Pops walked about with her enjoying the afternoon, for soon it would be dark with the winter days being so short. Right before twilight they went back inside to have some supper. After washing the dishes and completing their toilette, they were all ready to relax for the evening. In the dim battery operated light Muffin, Mum and Pops snuggled about the table together. The three of them sat in silence for a little bit just enjoying each others company.

Mum remarked out of the quiet, "Christmas is nice and it's good to see family but I sure am glad we don't have to go anywhere tomorrow."

Pops said, "Me too. Gives us more time to hang out with The Muffin!" Hearing this Muffin smiled a satisfied cat smile and purred so they would know she felt the same way.

Mum with a twinkle in her eyes said, " Muffin can you guess who's coming to visit tomorrow?"

Muffin gazing at them both thought, "Is it? Could it be?"

Pops smiled, "That's right Muffin. Vincent's coming to see us tomorrow!"

Her Cat smile grew bigger and her eyes lit up and glowed. "Vincent Yay Vincent!" Almost beside herself with happiness. "Meow!" She thought. She felt like doing Cat dances! Laying down to sleep that night with Mum and Pops. Muffin fell asleep dreaming of Vincent. ZZZ...purr...

They slept in the next morning. Getting up about the time it was getting light, Pops went outside to change the propane bottle since the other one had ran out of gas. He came back in saying, "You can turn the heater back on now and heat up the kettle." Muffin purred. "Yay for the kitty heater!"

Mum was saying, "Vincent plans to be here by noon. That gives us plenty of time to clean up the place and fix a nice simple meal to have together." So after breakfast the three got their tiny RV home ready for Vincent's first visit. Once it was in order Mum and Pops went outside with their tall yeti bottles full of warm water, shampoo and towels to wash their hair. Muffin had decided to take a bath too, wanting to look extra nice for Vincent. Coming back inside to comb their hair, Mum and Pops took turns washing up in the tiny bathroom. Afterwards having gotten dressed in clean clothes, everyone was ready and looking their best! Midmorning Mum's brother Phillip came by for a visit. So they talked with Phillip awhile. He asked if Colby had signed the easement paperwork also. Mum and Pops just shook their heads. Phillip with a sigh said, "Hope he decides to do it soon."

"Our thoughts exactly." Muffin thought.

They thanked him for letting them get water at Mum and Phillip's old home place. Getting into his truck to leave Phillip said, "Let me know if you need anything." Waving as he drove away, Muffin mused, "Boy, Mum's siblings sure are nice."

As noontime and Vincent's arrival approached, they went excitedly about preparing their meal. Muffin jumped up into the bedroom alcove to keep an eye out for his arrival. She had been watching steadily for half an hour when suddenly she saw him coming up the road. Slowing he turned onto the lane, then drove his car down to park it next to the Jeep. Vincent got out of his car as Mum and Pops with Muffin in his arms burst out of the RV to greet him. "Muffin!" He called, "It's so good to see you." Vincent handing Mum a bag he was carrying took Muffin from Pops as they went inside the RV for dinner.

Vincent stood holding Muffin while looking around as Mum and Pops checked out the bag of goodies he had brought for them. Yummy canned soups and tins of fishy snacks! Plus he had picked up a bag of gourmet cat food for The Muffin!" "Vincent is the best!" She purred. Having all three of her favorite humans in one place made her very happy.

While Mum put the finishing touches on dinner, Vincent still looking around remarked, "That they sure had done a nice job setting up the RV." Then they all sat down for their simple meal together with Muffin near them.

Vincent had made sure she got some of the new cat food. Muffin trying a bite sighed blissfully, "Yum! Good choice Vincent!" She jumped up onto the seat between Vincent and Mum when finished with her meal. "Ahh this is lovely." She purred listening to their conversation.

Vincent was very curious about the RV and asked lots of questions. Mum and Pops told him how the gas cook stove and heater worked, showed him the tiny bathroom and explained how they washed up and how it worked for bathroom use except for in the middle of the night. They also showed him their dishpan for washing dishes. He checked out all the handy storage. Looking in doors and drawers getting a feel for the place. As they opened the door to the RV fridge, Vincent looking inside exclaimed, "What? You've got canned goods in the refrigerator!" Laughing Mum and Pops explained that since they didn't have electricity yet food got colder in the cabinets than in the refrigerator. So they were using the refrigerator to keep some of their canned goods from freezing. Vincent mused, "Well I guess that makes sense. Never thought of it that way before. The fridge being thicker walled would be more insulated from the cold." Looking over at the bedroom alcove, He said, "I've got to try that out." Climbing up into it he lay down. "Ah this is comfy and very roomy too."

Muffin who had climbed up on to the bed with Vincent purred, "You're darn right it is!"

After giving him a tour of the RV on the inside, they all went outside to get some fresh air and wander about in the Walnut Grove. Vincent was not used to seeing Muffin outdoors there and was worried she might get lost. Mum and Pops reassured him that they kept a close eye on her. Muffin realizing Vincent was worried about her rubbed against his legs. She knew that all three of her humans always tried to take good care of her. They all walked over to the big beautiful Cedar tree that Vincent used to climb up into and read books. One time he had even climbed up to the top of the Cedar tree to put a Christmas star on top. Muffin hearing this story thought, "That must have been a very special day indeed! Vincent must be quite a climber. I wonder if maybe he really could be part Cat?

Since that's one of our specialties." This was yet another Cat trait that he had. Just like how he liked to sleep during the day. "Maybe someday Vincent would really grow fur after all." Muffin mused.

Next all of them walked over to look at the old house foundation. Vincent had never seen it cleared off before. He was impressed by how good of shape it was still in. He ask what the old house used to look like. Mum told him what she remembered about it. Pops commented that they were thinking of either building the cabin or the shop on top of the foundation. This reminded Vincent about the electricity. He asked, "Has Colby signed easement papers yet? How is that going?"

Mum replied, "Well, Colby's been dragging his feet on it. He thinks it will devalue his land."

Vincent remarked, "Why in the world would he think such a thing! Hopefully someone can talk some sense into him."

Pops answered, "We're sure working on it. With any luck he will decide on signing the papers soon!"

"Yes." Mum said, "We're trying to stay optimistic." Eventually they all meandered back to the RV. Vincent looked over the outside of it. Pops showed him where the propane bottle was stored plus the trapdoors for wiring and storage. Going back inside they sat down around the table. Muffin had a quick snack and litter box break before resuming her spot between Vincent and Mum.

Lying on her blanket she let Vincent, Mum and Pops' voices wash over her. "It just doesn't get any better than this!" Muffin purred. She listened as Mum and Pops asked how things were going for him in Springfield. Also asking him if there was any news of Brenden and Madison.

The time just flew by! Vincent suddenly realizing

that it would be dark soon, remarked he should probably head back to Springfield. Mum and Pops smiled saying, "We've sure enjoyed your visit! We will come down soon and visit you."

Muffin with her heart in her eyes watched Vincent avidly. Noticing he said, "Don't worry Muffin I will be back again soon to visit!"

"Whew." She sighed, "Thank goodness!" Waving, Vincent drove back up the lane and then off down the gravel road until out of sight. Waving in return Muffin, Mum and Pops walked back to the RV thinking of what a lovely day with Vincent it had been. After their dance of washing up and putting on comfy clothes for the evening, Mum turning on their battery powered lights ask, "How about a snack supper tonight?"

"Sounds good." said Pops.

"Me too." Muffin purred.

Laying out food for supper; Muffin, Mum and Pops sat down to enjoy their snacks enthusing about their lovely visit with Vincent! Knowing they would see him again soon, Mum and Pops wondered what the next step should be for tomorrow. Both of them wondering "if" they were going to hear from Colby. They talked quietly about what they would do if Colby didn't sign the easement papers. Neither one of them liking what they might be left with if they didn't get electricity. Pops sighing said, "I think we've talked enough about that for this evening."

Mum nodding replied, "I agree. Well it is almost the end of the year. Let's give it until New Year's Day and then call Colby."

Muffin blinked her eyes in agreement. "We'll be alright." She thought.

An hour later Vincent texted saying he had made it home safely and that he would be up to visit them again soon. "Give The Muffin a pat for me." He said.

That night as they all slept, Muffin dreamt about Vincent climbing the big Cedar tree. In her dream he was covered in fur and had claws with which to help him climb. When he made it to the top of the Cedar tree instead of a star he placed a flag with a little gray Cat on it that looked just like her. After he put the flag on top, Vincent let out a big meow before climbing back down the tree! ZZZ... purr... ZZZ... purr.

The next morning as Muffin, Mum and Pops woke up, Muffin still remembering her dream looked around to make sure she didn't see Vincent curled up in a corner somewhere purring like a Cat. "Wow! That was some powerful dream," She mused. Padding over to the side of the bed, Muffin jumped down just as Mum and Pops came back inside from bathroom duty. The three of them danced about, one to comb their hair, one to put the kettle on and one to use the litter box. Finishing their morning rituals Mum and Pops sat down with their cups of caffeine. Muffin after having some of the food and fresh water given her, jumped up onto the seat between them.

After breakfast, they told Muffin they were going to town for a few things and would stop to get some water. Muffin still feeling a bit tired yawned thinking, "O.k. Quiet time for this Cat!" So once Mum and Pops had gone, Muffin climbed up onto the table to watch the cows. She then saw in a field farther down some deer. She noted that they grazed like cows, but that she had never seen the cows jump the fence like deer did. A bit too heavy maybe? Having a snack and litter box break, Muffin then climbed up into the bedroom alcove. Kneading and purring about she settled down for a good Catnap. "Ahh." She smiled, "How comfy." zzz...

Muffin woke to the sound of Mum and Pops

coming down the lane. Parking the Jeep in front of the RV they carried water jugs into the RV and gave The Muffin a pat. Mum and Pops turning to go back outside said, "Come on Muffin you want to go?" Needing no further invitation she leapt out of the RV onto the ground.

She watched as they got large stones out of the back of the Jeep. Looking on as they arranged them in front of the RV door. Seeming happy with the results, Mum and Pops got two tarps out of the back of the Jeep with which to cover the vent holes on top of the RV. Then they stood back to survey their work. "Well done." thought Muffin.

Over the next several days Mum and Pops picked up tree limbs and cut tree sprouts around the place. Muffin would come along to supervise. Sometimes she would try to creep past them up the lane to the gravel road. But Mum and Pops always caught her, then they would chase her back down the lane towards the RV. "Whew!" panted Muffin, "Mum and Pops are a lot faster than I thought they would be!" She had tons of fun trying to sneak past them. Then there was the glory of the chase, as Mum and Pops ran after her back to the RV.

One morning they woke up to see an inch of snow on the ground! It sure was pretty! Plus the snow wasn't deep, so trips to the woods to answer the call of nature weren't bad either. Muffin enjoyed seeing all the colorful birds against the white of the snow outside. She went out to explore some even though her paws got cold in the snow. But Mum always dried Muffin well with a towel when she came back inside. There were visits from Mum's brother Scott who brought over an outdoor grill. Mum and Pops went to visit her sister Sue and her husband Ross. Mum's brother Phillip came over to make sure they were keeping warm enough. They also called Becky to see how she was doing. She was due to have the baby in early February. So her family hadn't been up to see their RV in the Walnut Grove yet. Muffin was enjoying getting to know Mum's family and some of the neighbors who came to visit.

With the end of December 2019 approaching, Mum and Pops told Muffin one day that they had decided to go look at pre-made cabins. Telling her they wanted to have a backup plan since Colby still hadn't been in contact with them. Muffin hoped that Mum and Pops heard something soon. Then they would know how to go about building a home here in their Walnut Grove. Coming back later from looking at pre-made cabins, Mum and Pops talked lightly about them and the various cabin types. Muffin listened attentively while lounging on the seat between them. "Well," said Pops, "I think from here on out until New Year's Day, we're going to focus on getting ready for our New Year's Eve celebration!"

"That's right," Mum replied, "The three of us will band together tomorrow and get this place in tiptop shape!"

Muffin upon hearing this thought, "That's the spirit. We'll have us a wild Cat time!" Mum turned on the battery powered lights. Pops gave The Muffin some of the fancy cat food Vincent had brought for her. Mum noticing got out a can of soup they also had gotten from Vincent and a tin of fishy treats as well to have with crackers. Muffin smelling the fish gave Mum the "What about me?" look. So she had fancy cat food and fish for supper. While eating, Mum and Pops went over what they would like to do tomorrow December 31 to get ready for New Year's Eve. Muffin listened intently excited for their party. They would clean and tidy the inside of the RV, pick up around the outside, plus dust the Jeep and arrange the things they kept inside of it. After going to Osceola to get a few treats for their party, they would sponge bath, wash their hair outside and then get dressed for their New Year's Eve celebration!" "Me too!" purred Muffin. "I'm going to give myself an extra good bath."

Having cleared away the supper dishes as they talked, Mum and Pops took care of their toilette then sat back down with Muffin in between them on her blanket. They gave her a good petting and then settled in to do word find puzzles. Mum and Pops had picked up a couple of them recently and enjoyed doing one or two of them in the evening. Muffin liked to watch them as they went about this pastime. First making faces as they searched for a word, then scratching noises with their ink pens as they circled the found word. Mum and Pops seemed to enjoy the word find puzzles and Muffin had a good time watching them. He he.

Laying in the bedroom alcove later that night, Muffin, Mum and Pops gazed up at the stars. "Oh what grand stars above us. They make my thoughts feel far." Mum sang.

With Pops chiming in, "With moonbeams of light to guide us. We'll follow them in the dark."

Muffin happy and comfy thought, "Well put." as she drifted off to sleep.

The next morning as they woke, Pops exclaimed, "It's the last good day of the year!"

Muffin let out a big "Meow, as Mum replied, "That's right. Let's make the most of it!" So they all sprang out of bed on springy deer feet to greet the day. It was a lovely morn with the sun coming up in the east. Clothes were donned, hair was combed and trips outside to the bathroom were made. Mum gave fresh food and water to The Muffin. She looked up at her with thankful eyes as she stepped into the litter box.

Pops put the kettle on for hot drinks. While the water heated he remarked that, "They should take the extra propane bottle to town to get a refill, then they could use the grill Scott had brought them. Plus it could be an extra bottle for the RV too, since the weather was getting cooler."

"Good idea." said Mum.

So after breakfast, they loaded the propane bottle and some laundry into the Jeep, then drove off to town to run errands. Muffin deciding to rest while they were away jumped up into the seating alcove to lie on her blanket. "Nap time for this Cat!" She purred. Mum and Pops came home a couple of hours later. Muffin watched as they unloaded bags of New Year's Eve goodies, clean laundry and a full propane bottle. Mum coming inside said, "Look Muffin we washed the Jeep! We vacuumed it too."

"Yay!" She purred, "The Jeep is festive too."

Pops came in from hooking up the propane bottle to the grill saying, "We're ready to grill some hot dogs now!"

Mum gathering the hot dogs, a fork, oil and foil for the grill replied, "Let's go. I'm hungry!" Muffin jumping out the RV door, walked over to hang out with Mum and Pops as they grilled the hot dogs. Soon the hot dogs were grilled and the three of them went inside to set out beans, chips and bread for their meal. Gathering the plates, silverware and condiments they sat down to eat. Pops cut up some small hot dog pieces for Muffin. But she could never decide if she liked hot dogs. She mostly enjoyed smelling them while they grilled. Mum knowing this had also given her some treats just in case.

Finishing their meal, Mum and Pops washed dishes and had a quick cup of joe, then with Muffin supervising they cleaned and tidied inside the RV. As Mum finished making the bed up with fresh sheets, she turned to Pops saying, "I'll take care of cleaning the bathroom if you will change the litter in Muffin's box."

Muffin hearing this thought, "Yay, a fresh litter box!"

Pops stepped back inside sitting down the fresh litter box a while later just as Mum had finished up the bathroom. "Come on Muffin," Pops said, "Let's go outside so Mum can sweep the floor." Muffin bounded out the door happily after him.

Mum joined them outside when she was finished. It was a lovely clear day. A little cool out but nice. The three walked up to the mail box together to check the mail. Muffin enjoyed their stroll up the lane. Gazing around Mum and Pops were very happy about how the Walnut Grove looked. Mum's brother-n-law Ross had brush-hogged it back in late October. Plus they had spent a lot of time since then picking up tree limbs and clearing off the old house foundation. All with The Muffin's supervision of course. The Walnut Grove with it's big beautiful Cedar tree as a focal point looked amazing! "When I think about what this place looked like before we started cleaning it up! Why the weeds were as tall as me." exclaimed Mum.

Muffin's eyes got huge when she heard this. "Wow!" She mused, "That's hard to imagine with how the place looks now." Talking as they meandered back to the RV, Mum and Pops tidied up the few things that were outside of it. While they worked, Muffin went under the RV to investigate and sniff about. They had just the right amount of stuff stored underneath for it to be interesting. Done with their task, Mum and Pops dusted the inside of the Jeep and arranged the belongings they had stored in there. Muffin starting to feel a nap coming on was glad to hear them call her to go inside. She dashed for the RV door and was the first one back inside.

After a quick snack Muffin settling onto her blanket in the seating alcove yawned, "Ahh nap time! I must rest before our New Year's Eve celebration." Noticing just before she closed her eyes that Mum and Pops were getting ready for their sponge bathes. It was getting late in the afternoon and they liked to finish washing their hair outside before it got dark. She fell asleep dreaming of their New Year's Eve party. ZZZ...purr...zzz...

Muffin woke with a start just as Mum came inside from having washed her hair. Pops was standing in front of the closet mirror combing his hair. As he was finishing, Mum traded him places. Pops looking out the window noticed that Colby's Mom was driving down the lane toward their RV. He exclaimed, "I wonder what she wants?"

Mum trying to comb out her hair muttered, "Hard to say. Is Colby with her?"

Pops replied, "It doesn't look like it. I'll go see what she wants. Come on outside when you're finished."

"Okay," she said.

Muffin more awake now thought, "I need to take my bath. It will be party time soon!"

Mum was still combing her hair a little while later when Pops stepped back inside the RV. Looking over at her he said, "Colby's Mom says he is not going to sign any easement papers. I think you need to come outside with me to talk to her now."

Mum looking guilty because she had been trying to go as slow as possible, hoping to avoid hearing what Colby's Mom had to say replied, "Alright. Let's go then."

Muffin jumped up into the bedroom alcove where she would have a view of Mum, Pops and Colby's Mom from the window. She could tell that the conversation with Colby's Mom was not going well. Mum and Pops were trying hard to be friendly and reason with her. But she just kept saying over and over again how they needed to see it from Colby's side. That light poles on his land would devalue it. Hearing this Pops made a point of saying, "Colby already had light poles on his land. Those light poles were what gave him electricity that also pumped water up from his well. Most people were just glad to have electricity so they could go about their daily lives!"

Mum shivering from having wet hair murmured, "How are we supposed to build our place without electricity?" Colby's Mom only keep repeating that they needed to understand how Colby felt. He wanted us to have electricity, but didn't want to sign the papers because it would devalue the land and the light company would be able to drive on his land anytime they wanted.

Pops in one last ditch effort stated, "The light company only came onto someone's land if they suspected that was where the problem was during a power outage. Most people were only too glad to let the light company's crew come on to their land then. That way their power could be restored!"

But Colby's Mom only began repeating the same thing over and over again. Mum standing up looked over at Colby's mom saying, "I'm going back inside, my hair's wet and I'm cold." Turning, Mum opened the RV door and stepped inside.

Pops spoke to Colby's Mom a few more minutes as she got back into her car. Then walking over to the RV he came inside as she drove away. Mum and Pops looked at each other, as they stood by the bed just inside the door. Mum was stroking Muffin's fur in an attempt to calm herself as much as to pet Muffin. "What are we going to do now?" She asked.

Pops looking a little menacing from anger but trying to stay calm answered, "I don't know yet. But we will think of something."

"That wasn't a very nice thing of her to do on New Year's Eve." Mum exclaimed, "Somehow we are going to have to rise above this."

Muffin still feeling a little bewildered by it all thought, "Let me at em'! I'll give them the tooth and the claw."

Pops rallying said, "We can't let them rain on our parade. It's New Year's Eve!"

Mum noticing that it was completely dark answered, "That's right. It's time we had our New Year's Eve snack feast! Right Muffin?"

Muffin jumping down out of the bedroom alcove meowed, "Let's get this party started!" Mum and Pops went into action laying out their party treats. Muffin hopped up onto her blanket in the seating alcove while they got the feast ready. Mum putting tasty tidbits on a paper plate for Muffin placed it on the floor. Then Pops and her filling their own plates sat down at the table, as Muffin made a beeline for her plate of goodies. Then they all began their New Year's Eve feast!

Enjoying their party snacks in the dim battery powered light, Pops commented, "I sure wish we could listen to some music for our celebration." Music was the one thing they missed in the RV.

Mum said with a smile, "Maybe we don't have a way to listen to music. But at least we have the moon and the stars."

"And how!" sighed Muffin looking out the window. After they had finished their snacks, Mum and Pops walking over to the sink cabinet filled their coffee cups with their special drink called "Muffin cups". They used their coffee cups for everything from water, to coffee and tea, to Muffin cups. And having no ice mixed their RV drinks straight.

Muffin after a litter box break and a drink of water, jumped up into the seating alcove just as they sat down. "Cheers!" Mum and Pops sang raising their RV drinks for a toast. "Cheers Muffin." Muffin smiled her Cat's smile to them. Though they were a little freaked out by this business with Colby, they were trying to maintain a positive outlook, all wanting to have a good New Year's Eve celebration. So they talked of past New Year's Eve gatherings. Mum texted her friends at Walnut Street Inn to say Happy New Year, to which her friends replied back quickly. Pops called Becky and then Vincent so they could wish them Happy New Year. They had both agreed not to tell Becky and Vincent just yet about Colby's decision. Muffin for her part enjoyed hearing Vincent's voice on the telephone, he would be coming to visit them again soon. Mum and Pops told lots of funny stories that night. Muffin snuggled on her blanket in between them, enjoyed their animated conversation and laughter. Mum and Pops knew how to roll with the flow! She knew they would find a way to have their cabin in the Walnut Grove. Midnight came and Mum and Pops with their cups raised high cried out, "Happy New Year! Happy New Year Muffin!"

Muffin having been dozing a little bit came wide awake with a start, "It's the New Year? Wow!"

The three of them stayed up a couple of more hours that night. Huddled together slightly because it was becoming cooler in the RV. Pops thinking for a minute said, "Maybe we should go look at those pre-made cabins again."

Mum pausing to consider replied, "Sounds like a good plan. Why don't we go tomorrow?"

Muffin with her eyes barely open now thought, "Way to go! I knew you two would think of something." Then completely worn out they crept off to bed. Soothed by the closeness of one another, they fell into a deep sleep. zzz...

BUILDING OUR LIFE
OLD STYLE

So tired they slept in the next morning. Waking up in broad day light, Muffin hearing the call of the litter box was the first one out of bed. Mum and Pops tumbled out of bed a few minutes later. "Good morning Muffin!" Mum said as she put out fresh food and water for her.

Pops coming back in from bathroom duty said, "It's starting to feel down right cold out there. Better make sure the propane bottle is pretty full."

Mum said with a shiver, "It's colder in here too. We will probably want to start wearing more clothes to keep warm in the RV. Lucky for Muffin she has a fur coat!"

Muffin hearing this thought, "I'm glad too. Wish Mum and Pops had a fur coat to stay warm." After a cup of joe and a bite to eat, Mum and Pops gave The Muffin a pat telling her they were going to look at pre-made cabins. Wish them luck! "Good luck!" She purred.

Pops loaded up an empty propane bottle as he started the Jeep. Mum just finishing getting ready for their trip gave Muffin some treats. "We will be back soon!" they told her before driving away. Still tired from their late night party, Muffin snuggled more comfortably on her blanket. Mum had even covered her with another blanket to keep her nice and toasty. Sighing she slipped off to kitty Cat dreamland. Purr...zzz...

Mum and Pops came back mid-afternoon. From up in the bedroom alcove Muffin saw them coming. For she had been bird watching, a most enjoyable pastime. They came inside saying, "Hi Muffin! Soon as we get our caffeine ready we will tell you about the cabins."

Cups in hand they all sat down. Pops said, "Looks like we're going to buy a barn style cabin, Muffin. We're going back in a couple of days to find out all of the details."

"That's right." Mum said smiling.

Muffin listened as Mum and Pops talked of using a handsaw, a battery powered skill saw and screw gun, plus an old fashioned hammer to complete the inside of the cabin. They brainstormed about which materials to use. They planned to buy some that could be cut and hammered the old way, without electricity. Pops said, "I think wafer board and tongue-n-groove pine car-siding would be good choices."

Mum chimed in, " Good! That will keep us from having to use sheetrock. It's messy and hard to clean up after."

"Well we can talk about it more later." Pops enthused.

Just then the phone rang and Mum answered it. It was her sister Sue asking if Colby had signed the easement papers yet. "No." Mum sighed, "Colby is not going to sign. So we're going to buy an Amish built barn cabin and finish it out without electricity."

Sue upon hearing this replied, "She couldn't imagine why he wouldn't sign the papers." Mum explained to her what Colby's Mom had told them. "Why that's ridiculous." Sue exclaimed, "Hey Ross has a battery powered skill saw and screw gun. I'll see if you can borrow them." Mum thanked her before hanging up the phone.

And so on it went, the very next evening Mum's brother Scott hearing about their situation through the sibling grapevine, came by to chat. After Mum and Pops told him their plans, Scott said, "I have a rainwater catchment tank you can have to use." He just shook his head over Colby's decision saying, "He's not going to make any friends around here by doing this."

Muffin was heart warmed by all of Mum's siblings support. When her brother Phillip came by to visit, they told him of Colby's decision, telling him they planned to finish out an Amish barn cabin without electricity, Phillip paused considering then said, "It's getting kind of cold out for you to be staying in an RV. If you want pull your RV down to the farm so you can plug it in for electricity, or you guys could live in the ole home place until you finish your cabin." Muffin, Mum and Pops were overwhelmed by Phillip's generosity. Thanking him repeatedly for the offer and would certainly let him know. As Phillip was leaving he called out, "By the way I have a ladder you can borrow."

"Thanks again Bro!" Mum sang out.

That evening mulling things over after supper Pops said, "I think we should go look at that barn cabin again tomorrow. If we still like it we should go ahead and buy it."

Muffin was all ears as Mum asked, "What do you think about Phillip's offer?"

Pops replied, "I'm still blown away by it. The thing is with having the RV already set up in the Walnut Grove, he would hate to have to move it again."

"There is that." Mum answered, "He also mentioned that the house needed a good cleaning. Plus a lot of stored furniture is in it that would need moved. Besides we would have to find a wood stove for heat." Muffin's eyes got huge just thinking about it! She sighed, "As much as I would like to live in my ole home place, at least to help clean it up a bit, it would make it even harder for us to work on the barn cabin."

Pops eyeing The Muffin and Mum asked, "Are you thinking what I'm thinking?"

Returning his stare Mum smiled saying, "Yes I think we are. Right Muffin?"

Muffin sitting up taller thought, "Whoa is this going to be an adventure all on its own or what! This will be the true Warrior Cat Way!

"It's settled then." Pops said, "Although I will take Phillip up on borrowing that ladder!"

Waking the next morning Muffin, Mum and Pops sprang out of bed on springy deer feet. Mum turned the gas cookstove on to heat up water. It doubled as an extra heat source in the tiny RV. Pops came in from having bathroom duty outside saying, "Whew it sure is brisk out!"

Muffin realized quickly the floor was cold everywhere except in front of the heater. So after breakfast she jumped up onto her blanket in the seating alcove. Mum covered her with another blanket as they sat down to have their cups of joe. "Today was the day!" Muffin smiled her Cat's smile, " Mum and

Pops are to going to buy the barn cabin." Soon as breakfast was eaten, Mum and Pops loaded up water jugs that needed refilled. Then giving her a pat told her they would be back this afternoon. Muffin excitedly rubbed against their legs!

After Mum and Pops had gone, she leapt up into the bedroom alcove to study the old house foundation. She could just imagine their cabin sitting there. It was going to be amazing! Muffin fell asleep dreaming of the cabin and all the adventures they were going to have.

She woke up later to see four deer grazing on the other side of the big Cedar tree. She loved to watch them flicking their tails while grazing. Suddenly something spooked them and the springy footed beast took off running and leapt over the fence, running until they were out of sight. "Magnificent." purred Muffin. "Such speed and agility!"

Mom and Pops came back late in the afternoon. They told Muffin all about the barn cabin. "We should have it here within the week." Pops exclaimed, "Then we should be able to finish the inside in four to six weeks!

"That's wonderful!" thought Muffin. They were all beginning to realize that wintertime in an RV could be rather cold. There also was the issue of the little gas heater creating moisture on the ceiling and walls inside of the RV. They had taken to covering the bed and seating area with plastic trash bags to protect them. "This is very exciting news!" Muffin purred. She had complete faith in Mum and Pops' ability to get it done.

Pops had taken measurements on the inside of the barn cabin. So now he could see how much insulation and wafer board was needed. "Why don't Muffin and you do some figuring while I fix us all supper." Mum offered.

"Sounds like a plan!" Pops replied. Muffin smiled her Cat's smile. Even though she had been feeling a bit under the weather with her tummy lately, she was still a part of all this and tried to stay as involved as possible. By the time Mum had their supper ready, Pops was done with his figures with The Muffin's supervision. Sitting down to supper He said, "Let's take this list to town tomorrow. See what kind of quote they will give us."

"O.k." Mum replied.

"That's right!' Muffin meowed, "Let's keep the ball rolling!"

They spent the rest of the evening relaxing together. Muffin, Mum and Pops being very adaptable had discovered by watching that only certain areas on the seating alcove and bed got wet from the moisture dripping. So they just didn't sit in those spots. It seemed they were able to go with the flow more these days. Their sleeping arrangements were not always the same either. Muffin sometimes slept on her blanket in the seating alcove. Or at times on the floor in front of the heater. Every once in awhile she slept with Mum and Pops. She just had to make sure and find a dry spot. They all knew that they would appreciate the barn cabin even more because of this experience.

Vincent called asking if it was still alright to come up and see them tomorrow? Hanging up the phone Mum and Pops said brightly, "Sure glad Vincent reminded us about tomorrow, we will pick up something yummy to eat in town tomorrow!"

"Yay Vincent's coming to visit!" Muffin purred.

They were all happy and excited to see him. The following morning Mum and Pops were getting out of bed just as Muffin jumped down from her sleeping spot in the seating alcove. All three of them were extra peppy this morning. Between knowing they would be getting their barn cabin soon and Vincent coming to visit, not even the colder weather could bring them down! Mum and Pops dressing a little finer with Vincent coming, drank their caffeine in record time. Muffin just beginning to get her eyes totally open noted all of this. "Me thinks I will give myself a good bath while Mum and Pops are away!" She mused.

They dashed off to town to get a building materials quote, plus pick up some yummy food for Vincent's visit. Muffin deciding she would bathe in front of the heater, settled in for a good bath. Afterwards she got up on the table to watch the cows for awhile. Mum and Pops arriving back around 11am let Muffin out for some fresh air. She sniffed about under the Jeep and RV. Looking around she saw squirrels running around near the Walnut trees. They were such funny little beasts! As Mum and Pops finished unloading the Jeep they called, "Come on Muffin let's go get ready for Vincent!"

Going inside the RV, Mum began preparing their meal, tidying up the place a little while she was at it. Pops was telling Muffin all about how they had gotten a really good quote on what they needed to start work on the barn cabin. They would be placing an order soon. "Yahoo!" Muffin thought, "Good news!"

She realized she was beginning to smell good food, just as she saw Vincent driving up the gravel road. Mum scooped Muffin up into her arms as Pops opened the door and they stepped outside to meet him. Vincent parking beside the Jeep opened his car door with some good ole Trevor Hall music still playing on his stereo. "Well hello there!" He said with a smile. Mum handed Muffin to Vincent while Pops and her saying hello asked if he had a good trip. As they went inside the RV, Vincent while still holding The Muffin sat down to pet her as they all talked. "So how's everything going? He asked. Will you be getting electricity soon?" Mum and Pops had not told him sooner wanting to tell him in person about this, so they explained the situation with Colby. Vincent got about as mad as they had ever seen him. He just couldn't believe it. "What are you going to do now?" Vincent asked as he stroked Muffin's fur.

"Well." Pops said, "For starters we bought an Amish built barn cabin yesterday, which has two sleeping lofts. It will be delivered and set up here sometime this week. We also have a quote for some building materials to finish out the inside of it."

Vincent hearing this news asked where they had bought the cabin. Mum and Pops showed him a picture of the barn cabin. Then Mum described the inside layout of the barn cabin to him. "But how are you going to finish the inside without electricity?" Vincent wondered. Pops mentioned all of the hand tools and battery powered tools they would use. Mum explained how Phillip, Sue and Ross, plus Scott and Melonie had been offering them other useful things too. Vincent was very heartened by this. Muffin gave his hand a lick to let him know they would be alright. "Well." He replied, "You certainly have gotten some of this figured out that's for sure."

Mum filling Muffin's bowls said, "Time to eat! We can talk more about it then." As Muffin, Vincent, Mum and Pops enjoyed their meal together Vincent asked more detailed questions about the barn cabin. Then he exclaimed. "But what about music? You have to be able to play music!" All four of them loved music.

Pops replied, "Right now we can hear it in the Jeep or we can play live acoustic music."

Vincent his mind scrambling for some sort of solution said, "It will take me some time, but I can put you together a mini stereo set up that's solar powered."

"Really!" Mum exclaimed, Wow! "That sounds amazing! Let us know how much money you need to get your idea started."

Later after their meal Muffin, Vincent, Mum and Pops went outside for a stroll. Walking over to the old house foundation Pops told Vincent they were going to place the barn cabin right on top of it. Looking around Vincent said he had just never realized how beautiful it was here in the Walnut Grove.

Everyone agreed that it was even more lovely than they had remembered. "We sure are lucky." Muffin thought.

As he was leaving in the late afternoon Vincent said, "Keep me up on everything that's going on! I'll be back up again next weekend."

Pops sang out, "The barn cabin should be delivered by then. You'll be able to check it out!"

"Sounds good." Vincent called out. Then he drove up the lane as Muffin, Mum and Pops looked on. The three were already looking forward to his next visit.

Over the next several days they waited excitedly to hear when the barn cabin would be delivered. Pops called in an order for the concrete blocks that were needed for extra foundation support. The order was delivered that day! Mum and Pops also began gathering the hand tools needed for building. Sue and Ross brought over the battery powered skill saw and screw gun thankfully. A couple of days later Phillip and Scott each brought a ladder for them to use. Muffin was very curious about the ladders and had to give them a thorough investigation. She supposed they could be useful if you didn't have claws to climb with.

That night all three of them woke up around 1pm realizing it was colder in the RV than usual. Mum glancing down at the heater said, " I think the propane bottle must be empty." So Pops eyes only halfway open got out of bed and stumbled outside in the dark to change propane bottles. Then coming back in he turned the heater on again before getting back in bed! Brrr...

On Tuesday morning January 7th the place with the barn cabin called saying they could deliver it the following day. Muffin, Mum and Pops became very excited upon hearing this and done Cat dances of joy! After their Cat dances Pops called in the order for insulation and wafer board. He got off the phone saying it would be delivered that afternoon. Yay!

"Man, things are really starting to happen!" Muffin purred. So Mum and Pops drove to town to pick out the nails, screws and staples that would be needed to get started. Arriving back at 12:30pm, Mum and Pops having eaten some broasted chicken already had brought some back for The Muffin. "It smells wonderful." She purred, deciding to have a small snack of it now and save the rest for another meal. It was better for her tummy. She rubbed against Mum and Pops legs in appreciation of the chicken.

Just as they were finishing their midday cups of joe, Pops noticed the lumber truck coming up the road with their insulation and wafer board. Mum said, "Looks like it's time to do some unloading." So they began putting on coats and shoes to go outside and help unload. Muffin feeling kind of tired after eating chicken stayed in for a nap. Mum covered her up with a blanket before they went outside.

Later after unloading, Mum and Pops came back in the RV. Sitting down with Muffin they rested while she napped. Talking quietly while they warmed up so Muffin could have a nice long nap, for they knew napping after meals helped her tummy. An hour later she woke up just as Pops said, "Feels like it's going to be a cold one tonight."

Looking out the windows Mum replied, "Going to get dark earlier too with it being so overcast." Muffin stretching as she stood up looked out the windows at the clouds. As one they began preparing for the evening. Doing what personal clean up was necessary and going outside to use the bathroom. By mutual agreement they decided on a snack supper. Then changing into comfy clothes, Muffin, Mum and Pops snuggled together for warmth and comfort in the dim light. They done a few word finds and tried to read in the faint light which was not a very easy thing to do. A couple of hours later with all three of them yawning, they went off to bed happy their barn cabin would be arriving tomorrow.

Waking the next morning around first light, Muffin, Mum and Pops lay in bed for awhile. With the weather becoming colder Mum would sometimes crawl out of bed long enough to turn the heater up and then climb back in bed where they all could stay warm while the RV heated up some more. There was much talk about the barn cabin. Today was the day it would be delivered! Muffin had been dreaming about it all night. She was very curious about what it looked like, for pictures to cats didn't make much sense. As long as it wasn't a round house it would be fine with her. Vincent, Mum and Pops had promised her it wouldn't be, thankfully.

They eventually got out of bed and went about their morning rituals. With the temperatures getting colder now, the trips to the woods to answer the call of nature were most daunting. Mum and Pops always came back looking pretty cold from those trips. Muffin sometimes wished they had a litter box too. After breakfast she climbed up onto her blanket to lie between Mum and Pops while they sipped nice hot drinks. Pops thought it would be noon to 1pm before the cabin was delivered. They had already cut a few tree limbs along the lane, thinking the barn cabin might hit them otherwise. Having decided to wait and see if it would fit through the gate, knowing they could remove the fencing quickly if necessary to widen the gate entrance.

So Muffin, Mum and Pops had a lazy morning together. Only going to get water down the road. Muffin was thoroughly enjoying Mum and Pops hanging out. She got lots of extra attention that way. Meow! A little after 11am Mum fixed them a light meal to eat before the barn cabin arrived. Pops went outside with Muffin following to do a last minute once over of the lane and the foundation, to make sure nothing had been forgotten. They came back inside just as Mum was ladling soup into bowls. Crackers and cheese were on the table. She had replenished Muffin's bowls for her adding a few treats as well, so they sat down to have a meal together. The water was being heated for caffeine when the building place called saying they would be there by 1 to 1:30pm. "Yahoo!" Tonight they would celebrate. This was the first step in making their cabin dream come true! Close to 1:30pm they seen the barn cabin coming up the gravel road. "Whoa." thought Muffin with big eyes, "It looks huge!"

Mum and Pops talking at once as they threw on coats and shoes ask, "You want to come outside to watch Muffin?"

Her eyes still wide at the sight of the barn cabin. Muffin stared at them thinking, "If it's all the same to you I'll watch from inside the RV!"

Mum noticing how she felt said, "O.k. We will be back in a little while." Then Pops and her bolted out the door running up the lane to where the big truck with the barn cabin loaded on the back of its trailer sat waiting.

The man getting out of the truck said, " I'm not sure if I can back through this gate opening it looks pretty small but I will give it a try." Pops and him soon realized that wasn't going to work. While trying the man backed into the mailbox post. Whoops! As they talked about where the barn cabin was going to be set up, Mum, Pops and the driver walked down the lane to show him the old house foundation. Muffin looked on from her spot in the bedroom alcove. She watched as they walked back up the lane towards the road, wondering how they would get the barn cabin down the lane. It looked huge! The man walking over to the trailer unhooked some straps that secured the barn cabin saying, "Looks like I'm going to have to use the mule." Mum and Pops stood by watching with a chainsaw on hand in case Pops had to cut a fencepost out. The man walking back up to the cab of the truck reached inside and done something. The next thing Muffin, Mum and Pops knew the trailer started going up in the front and down in the back. Along with this the barn cabin free from its straps began to slide off the back of the trailer. As they looked on the man stopped the trailer's motion. Then climbing up into the truck he pulled it slowly forward until the barn cabin slid completely off of the trailer and was sitting in the middle of the gravel road!

"Well." Mum laughed, "looks like we're going to be living in the middle of the road, huh."

"That's right." Pops chuckled, "Everyone will just have to drive in the ditch to get around or go another way! Ha ha."

Then the man getting back out of the truck went over to a small machine he called the "mule" that was also on the trailer." He started it up and then driving it to an end of the barn cabin lifted up one side and then the other attaching hook on tires. After getting that side done, he drove over to the other side putting tires on it as well.

"Wow!" thought Muffin, Mum and Pops. Having never seen such a thing.

Looking over the gate opening again the man said, "You know I think you better widen that up a bit." So Pops with a chainsaw, a few other tools and Mum's help made the opening larger. Once finished Mum and Pops began walking slowly down the lane. The man still using the "mule" got on one side of the barn cabin and then the other jockeying it about until he had it in line with the gate opening. Then getting on the back side of the barn cabin he got the levers on the "mule" up under it lifting the cabin up and then began driving it down the lane. The barn cabin just cleared the gate opening as he drove through.

They had never seen anything like it! Pops was taking pictures as Mum went running back to the RV to share the moment with Muffin. "What do you think of that?" She asked excitedly, "Almost looks like the barn cabin is driving itself down the lane!" Before dashing back out the door again.

"Wow!" Muffin mused, "That's the craziest thing I've ever seen." Just as it came into full view around the tiny curve in the lane beside the huge Cedar tree, it seemed to grow even more. But whew! At least it had made it between the huge Cedar tree and the Walnut trees that were on the other side of the lane. Now the man and his "mule" had to pull the barn cabin forward facing south and back it up onto the old house foundation. Muffin, Mum and Pops all watched barely breathing while he just cleared a large Walnut tree limb with almost no room to spare.

Mum once again came running back into the RV shouting, "Would you look at that Muffin. He's almost got it over the top of the old house foundation!"

"Amazing!" purred Muffin, "I had no idea mules looked like that. I thought they looked kind of like a horse. They sure are strong!" Mum went back outside just as the barn cabin was fully placed on top of the foundation. Pops was talking with the man. Then the man started using the concrete blocks to set up and level the barn cabin. Every once in a while he would use his "mule" to help him raise or reposition it.

Finally about an hour before dark the man got the barn cabin totally set up. As he was leaving, Mum and Pops followed him back up the lane to his truck. Looking over at the mailbox post he had damaged the man said. "I think I can fix that." Within minutes he had it looking good as new. They thanked him for everything, then the man with his "mule" once more back on the trailer drove off down the gravel road.

Mum and Pops walked back to the RV marveling about how great the barn cabin looked on the old foundation. Opening the RV door Pops called, "Come on Muffin let's go check out the barn cabin!"

She jumped out the door in a flash, walking over with them. "Looks like it's always been there. Doesn't it?" mused Mum.

Pops scooped Muffin up in his arms as they went inside. Muffin looking around really liked how spacious and open it was with the high ceiling. Plus there were two lofts! "Way to go Mum and Pops!" She thought smiling her Cat's smile.

With darkness almost upon them they stepped back outside, standing on the porch a moment so they could enjoy the view. Strolling back to the RV in the twilight Pops sang out, "Let's have a quick wash up and get on with our celebration snack feast and party."

"Right on!" cheered Mum.

Muffin purring happily thought, "I'm ready for a wild gypsy Cat time!"

That evening as Muffin, Mum and Pops feasted and celebrated, they glowed with a warmth that had nothing to do with the heater. They radiated a joy that came with knowing their barn cabin now rested on the old house foundation.

Mum and Pops felt they should be able to have it move in ready in 4 to 6 weeks. Even without electricity they thought it should be ready enough by then. "We will have wood heat too! Which will keep us extra warm." Pops enthused. Muffin who didn't know anything about wood heat, loved the idea of extra warmth. Snuggled together in the dim light of an oil lamp they had just purchased they celebrated, Mum and Pops with "Muffin Cups" in hand toasted the three of them's upcoming latest adventure! Becky and Vincent had texted earlier to hear about the barn cabin delivery. Vincent would be coming up Saturday and so would be seeing it first hand. Turning in around midnight, Muffin, Mum and Pops slept well knowing that their barn cabin had arrived!

Getting up at 7am the next morning, Mum lit the new oil lamp then she put the kettle on. Pops coming back inside from bathroom duty said, "It feels a bit moist out there. Good thing we're moving the insulation and wafer board into the barn cabin today."

Muffin finishing a light breakfast jumped up onto her blanket. Feeling a little groggy they all sat in silence as Mum and Pops drank their morning cups of joe. Knowing it would take awhile for the temperature to raise outside, they didn't have breakfast until 9am.

Putting on layers of clothes afterwards, Mum and Pops gave The Muffin a good petting before going outside. The sunlight was very dim with clouds floating around and it was still cold out. They would have to keep moving to stay warm.

Muffin having gone outside briefly earlier with Mum and Pops had decided to stay in by the heater and take a nap. "Brr." She drowsed, "This Cat's going to stay warm by the kitty heater!" zzz...

Working steadily they managed to move 42 sheets of wafer board and numerous rolls of insulation into the barn cabin by mid afternoon. They checked in on Muffin several times, warming themselves while having a quick snack with her too. Then it was all about moving the work tools into the barn cabin.

By the time 4 o'clock rolled around Mum and Pops walking up to check the mailbox decided to call it a day. While slowly strolling back towards the RV, Mum yawning hugely murmured, "I'm ready for some Muffin time."

Nodding his agreement Pops replied, "Me too!"

Muffin had been watching them as they walked ever so slowly towards the RV. "Poor Mum and Pops, I'm giving them Cat care tonight. They look totally worn out!" She meowed. So lucky for Mum and Pops they had The Muffin for tender loving Cat care time. From the moment they walked in, Muffin was there rubbing against their legs. Mum in appreciation gave Muffin some of the special cat food from Vincent. While she heated soup up Pops pet The Muffin. After supper and changing into comfy clothes the three of them lounged about together in warmth and comfort. Muffin began purring and kneading on them as they both sighed and pet her more. This was the ultimate of The Muffin's Cat care time. With her delivering a calming state of zen to Mum and Pops! They went bonelessly off to bed that evening, covering her up with a blanket at the foot of the bed. Then giving The Muffin a final pat they fell into a deep sleep still hearing her purring in their ears.

Rain woke them up the following morning before first light. Since it was raining; Muffin, Mum and Pops lay about and slept in. Getting up at 7:30am it was cloudy and still raining. They three took their time with morning rituals. Mum took good care Muffin's food bowls before Pops and her sat down to have caffeine. When Muffin jumped up to lie between them, they gave her an extra good petting in appreciation of all the superior Cat care she had given them. What a Cat!

They enjoyed the oil lamp's light and heat as they slowly woke up. With it raining Mum and Pops couldn't cut insulation and wafer board outside on the barn cabin porch like they wanted to. So they would just have to do other things today. Muffin, Mum and Pops happened to be very good at rolling with the flow. So it was decided that they would go into town and run errands. Muffin was out of Temptations for pete sakes! Maybe they would go to the library. Then Mum and Pops would have some of that yummy broasted chicken! Saving some to bring back for The Muffin in thanks of her wonderful Cat care! She loved it when they brought home broasted chicken for her!

Mum and Pops drove off saying they would be back between 1 and 2pm. The Muffin feeling tired from all of the care she had given, fell off to sleep dreaming of broasted chicken! Yum...zzz...

She felt much more rested by the time they arrived back home. Standing on the ledge step of the bedroom alcove so she could greet them as they came in, Pops gave The Muffin a good petting while

Mum put a few things away. Then she got out the promised broasted chicken and cut some into small pieces for her. Muffin made a beeline for the chicken enjoying her poultry treat, eating only a small amount, since her tummy stayed in better shape that way. Besides it lasted her longer.

Mum and Pops hung out with The Muffin for awhile then walked over to the barn cabin to decide on how to begin with the interior work. They were just finishing up their discussion when the phone rang. Answering it Pops said to Mum, "It's Jeff!" Then he went outside to walk up and down the lane while talking to him. Mum headed over to the RV to keep Muffin company.

Half an hour later Pops came in saying Jeff was back from Montana. He was staying with his Mom. His brother Kenny had passed away and he was helping his Mom make arrangements. Mum and Pops hadn't had a chance to tell Jeff they were back in St. Clair county. Upon hearing, he then asked if he could come out for a visit that evening. Pops of course had said yes. Mum asked, "Did you tell Jeff we don't have electricity? It will be hard for him to see our place after dark."

Pops replied, "Nope! Jeff will figure it out."

So they went about straightening up the RV. Then gave themselves a thorough clean up too. By then it was completely dark outside. After having a light supper they sat down together to await Jeff's arrival. Muffin remembered Jeff coming to visit them before they moved. He had even spent the night. Several hours passed without Jeff making an appearance. Mum and Pops began to wonder if he might not make it out after all. Pops was napping over his reading when the phone rang around 9:15pm with Mum taking the call. It was Jeff asking if he could still come out to visit? He was running behind a bit. Pops awake now nodded yes when Mum looked over his way. So She said, "Sure come on out."

About 10pm Mum and Pops saw car lights coming up the road. Donning coats and shoes, they grabbed a battery powered lantern as they went out the RV door and up the lane. Jeff kind of knew where they were, but in the dark he couldn't tell exactly where the lane was at. But seeing the dim lantern light and then them, he turned and drove on down the lane. Greetings were exchanged, then Mum and Pops asked how he was doing, telling him how sorry they were about his brother Kenny. Jeff filled them on Kenny and his Mom. They let him know about their situation, taking him inside the barn cabin, he had no trouble figuring out they didn't have electricity. It was very dark in there with only the dim battery powered lantern light.

Coming back outside, they all walked over to the RV. Jeff noticing The Muffin gave her a pat. He said, "You know I think Muffin is the only Cat I haven't been allergic to. I didn't have any allergies when I stayed the night with you at your other place." Muffin, Jeff, Mum and Pops sat down in the alcove around the table and talked until midnight. He had lots of good ideas for them related to their current living situation, assuming the lack of utilities was only temporary. They went ahead and told Jeff about how Colby wouldn't sign easement papers. Jeff was furious. He cast a dark look over in the direction of where Colby lived.

Seeing this Pops said, "Well it's bound to come out alright in the end I imagine."

As Jeff was leaving that night Mum and Pops again told him how sorry they were to hear about his brother. They also thanked him for all of his good advice. With him saying he should be back this summer, he drove up the lane and then off down the gravel road.

Coming back inside the RV, Mum and Pops noticed Muffin was asleep on her blanket in the seating alcove. So covering her up with another blanket, they got ready for bed. Pops said, "Vincent's coming tomorrow! He will get to check out the barn cabin."

"He sure will!" said Mum, Muffin will be so happy to see him."

Waking up around 8am the next morning after their late night visit with Jeff, they got dressed and put the kettle on. Mum sang out, "Vincent's coming today!"

Muffin looking up from eating her breakfast thought, "Ah lovely! This will be a grand day indeed if Vincent is coming to visit." They took their time getting around knowing he wouldn't be there until 1pm. Since they had cleaned up the night before there wasn't really anything to do before he arrived. Mum and Pops even had the brilliant idea to have Vincent pick up pizza and chips at The Pilot on his way up! So their meal was already taken care of.

Seeing Mum's brother Phillip coming up the road around noontime, Mum and Pops stepped out to greet him. Phillip had parked his truck just inside of the gate since the lane was a little soft from a rain the day before. He was walking down the lane towards them. "Thought I better not pull the truck down it's pretty heavy." He said.

Mum and Pops replied, "Good idea! We probably won't be pulling down much longer either. Come on in and check out the barn cabin." Phillip gave the barn cabin a thorough once over outside then they went inside for him to have a look while they visited.

Around 1pm they were still talking when Vincent came driving up the gravel road. Seeing the truck parked up near the gravel road, he decided to go ahead and park on the shoulder of the road. Getting out of the car as he slung his backpack over a shoulder, then with pizza and chips in toll started walking down the lane. He had on a ball cap and was smiling.

Mum coming out of the barn cabin called, "Hi there! Hope you had a good trip. Thanks for picking up the pizza and chips!"

Vincent still smiling answered, "Yes he did have a good trip! And no problem on the pizza and chips."

"Your Uncle Phillip is in the barn cabin. Come see him and check it out before we eat." She said.

Vincent coming inside greeted his Uncle Phillip and Pops. While everyone chatted Vincent looked over the barn cabin. Realizing they would be eating soon Phillip said his goodbyes. They followed him out waving as he headed back up the lane to his truck. They couldn't talk him into staying to have a meal with them.

Muffin had been watching from the bedroom alcove, so she seen them walking towards the RV. "Yahoo it's Vincent time!" She purred. Pops opened the RV door and let Mum and Vincent in ahead of him. Vincent handing Mum the pizza and chips swept Muffin up into his arms talking to her all the while. He sat down with her at the table as Mum and Pops got them set up for their pizza feast! Mum also gave Muffin some of the broasted chicken she loved. What a wonderful time they had! With the company being enjoyed even more than the pizza. Muffin felt like a queen as Vincent pet her while visiting with Mum and Pops. He was happy to have gotten to visit with his Uncle Phillip too. They filled him in on Jeff's visit the night before also.

After having a cup of joe, the four of them went outside to check out the barn cabin. Vincent really liked it remarking that he would eventually like to put something on the property. Becky and him knew they could have their own place there if they wanted. Everyone thought that would be really cool!

The rest of their day together was sublime. Vincent ask lots of questions about how Mum and Pops were going to do the inside work on the barn cabin. Pops told him their ideas so far. With Mum commenting that what they didn't know they would figure out as they went along. Muffin listening to their conversation thought, "You got that right!"

Noticing it was almost twilight by then Vincent said he better head back home. He gave The Muffin another pat and then Mum and Pops a group hug. Walking up the lane to his car. Vincent called out, "I'll be back next week!"

"Sounds good to us!" They said smiling. "Drive safe."

Mum and Pops waved as Vincent drove off down the gravel road. Then they walked back down the lane. Muffin had watched him leave from the bedroom alcove so could see Mum and Pops as they came down the lane towards the RV.

After finishing their toilette and changing into evening clothes in record time, they decided to have a lazy evening together. Mum and Pops ate some leftover pizza, while Muffin had broasted chicken with some of that fancy cat food Vincent had brought for her. In the dim oil lamp light they enjoyed their meal while talking about his visit.

Afterwards stepping outside to brush their teeth and go to the bathroom, they settled back in around the table to give Becky a call to see how they were doing and tell her all about the barn cabin. They planned to go down for a visit soon. Being 8 months pregnant she needed to stay close to home. Hanging up the phone Mum and Pops pet The Muffin for awhile. All of them were feeling pretty zen like. Vincent texted to say he had made it back home safely. Then each pulling out a word-find book, Mum and Pops did a couple. Muffin always felt pretty entertained watching them make faces looking for the words then making scratching sounds with their ink pens as they circled a word. "He he. Mum and Pops sure are funny sometimes." She mused. Going to bed that night, they told her work on the barn cabin would begin tomorrow. Muffin settling down to sleep in front of the heater purred, "That sounds wonderful!" zzz...

The following morning Muffin, Mum and Pops rose early. They wanted to be wide awake and fully ready by the time it got first light out. Without having electricity they would need to make good use of all their daylight hours. Wanting to make sure The Muffin was well taken care of, she was let outside for some fresh air while they brushed their teeth and took turns making treks to the woods. Dressing well for the cold Mum and Pops gave The Muffin a final pat as she was laying down for a nap. Then they were off to begin work on the barn cabin!

Upon entering Mum and Pops realized they would need to move the rolls of insulation to begin. Since the wind outside was pretty cold they decided to cut the insulation inside after all. There may have not been any heat inside the barn cabin, but at least there wasn't any wind either. They would just have to keep moving to try to stay warm. Their plan was to insulate the walls first, so they began rolling out the insulation and cutting it to length. As they started fitting the pieces one at a time in between the wall studs, Pops stapled as Mum helped hold it in place while shining a flashlight so he could see. It might have been daylight outside; but inside the barn cabin it was dim and shadowy. After a while they developed a pretty good flow. Cutting then installing the insulation. Lucky for them hanging insulation on the walls wasn't too messy of a job. If careful they shouldn't get too much of it on them.

Every hour or so they took a bathroom break. Then Mum and Pops went inside the RV to warm up and see how Muffin was doing. They pet her, freshened up her food bowls and sometimes let The Muffin out if she was near the door when they came in. Then while Mum and Pops warmed up, Muffin would investigate around and underneath the RV. It gave her a chance to eat some grass and get an even closer look at all of the wildlife and those cows. Muffin enjoyed these outdoor romps.

By the time noon rolled around Mum and Pops were ready to eat! Working in the cold made you hungry that's for sure. She heated up some soup, while he sliced summer sausage and cheese. Mum put the food on the table while Pops gave Muffin some broasted chicken, then grabbing some crackers they sat down. After their meal, Muffin lay between them on her blanket while Mum and Pops had their cup of caffeine. Then giving The Muffin a pat they went back over to the barn cabin to work for the rest of the afternoon.

By 4 o'clock Mum and Pops had the walls mostly finished. Heading back over to the RV, they took off their hats to brush their hair. Luckily their hats had protected them some. Then also removing their coats, gloves and shoes they shook everything out well.

Leaving them to air, they went inside the RV to

heat up water for washing up. Sponge bathing to get the worst of the insulation off, their toilette was finished and comfy clothes put on. Pops then brought their outerwear and shoes back inside. Mum fixed some mac-n-cheese for supper, giving Muffin some fancy Cat food in her bowl before they sat down to eat.

Later after supper, Mum's sister called to see how they were doing. Sue and Ross had also been by to see the barn cabin. Mum told her they had insulated most of the walls that day and would be starting in the lofts tomorrow. Sue told her if they wanted to come by and take a shower tomorrow night to feel free. Mum thanked her saying they sure appreciated it. So now they could take a real shower too. Yah! Muffin, Mum and Pops lounged about the rest of the evening just enjoying each others company. The three of them turning in early that night to get plenty of rest for insulating the lofts tomorrow.

The following morning they were up early again. By the time it was daylight their morning rituals had been completed. Muffin had even been outdoors for some romp time. Mum and Pops with all their layers of clothes on, covered Muffin with a blanket for her nap.

Going over to the barn cabin they went about setting up for insulating a loft. But first they had to make room for the ladder they would need to get up into the south loft. Then Mum went up the ladder first into the loft with Pops handing up rolls of insulation before he also came up into the loft. They unrolled and cut to size the pieces of insulation on the loft floor. It being a sleep loft it was only four and a half foot tall at its highest point. Which meant you couldn't fully stand up but must crawl around in order to put a piece of insulation between the rafters. They both had to get under a piece then Mum would go forward pushing upward and holding onto the insulation, while also holding on Pops would staple it in place. So they were either really low on the sides of the loft, or pushing up while crawling or squatting. Needless to say it was quite a workout!

Mum and Pops worked up in the south loft all morning. Every once and awhile they would carefully climb down to take a break, each holding the ladder for the other. Mum and Pops let Muffin outdoors every so often. They had decided not to let her back in the barn cabin until finished with the insulation. Mum and Pops wanted to air it out and sweep up any scraps so The Muffin wouldn't get it all over her.

By noontime they had gotten all the insulation hung in the south loft. Whew! Those last two sections on each side of the peak had been kinda scary. They were close to the very end of the loft which was open to the floor below. It was hard to keep the insulation where it needed to be and not fall out of the loft! Making their way carefully back down the ladder, Mum and Pops walked over to the RV. As Pops opened the door, Muffin jumped to the ground ready for some outdoor time. They gave her a quick petting before going inside to fix their meal. She was hanging out by the Jeep when Mum opened the RV door calling, "Time to eat, Muffin!" Later they all three went outside to stroll around, walking up to check the mail while they were at it.

Then coming back inside the RV they made sure Muffin had everything she might need. Then heading off to the barn cabin they moved the ladder over to the north loft, before beginning the same process all over again. By scooting, squatting and crawling they managed to get the insulation up in the north loft., once more without falling out! They cleaned up all of the insulation scraps and also left some windows open to air out the barn cabin. Feeling totally covered in insulation from crawling beneath it all day, Mum and Pops were very thankful they would be getting a shower at Sue and Ross' house that evening.

Closing the door at 4:30pm Mum and Pops walked over to the RV. Letting Muffin outdoors with them, they decided to strip down outside since no one was around. After shaking their hair out, they went inside to wash up in the tiny bathroom. Putting fresh clothes on afterwards, Pops took a large bag outside to put all the dirty clothes in. He then put the bag of laundry in the Jeep to wash next time they went to town. They wouldn't be insulating again until they had came up with a ladder tall enough to reach the cathedral ceiling.

Mum had their meal ready by then so they sat down to eat. They gave Muffin lots of attention knowing they would soon be leaving to go take a shower at Sue and Ross' house . Then getting ready to go, Mum and Pops said they would be back in a couple of hours.

Muffin watching them drive off thought, "Poor Mum and Pops! They looked worn out and were scratching like they had the fleas. Plus their eyes were terribly red." She sure hoped a shower would make them feel better. Whew! Muffin decided she had best give herself a bath, just on the off chance that Mum and Pops did have the fleas. She didn't want red eyes like that either. Yikes! After a very thorough bath she lay in the bedroom alcove listening to the owls hoot and the coyotes howling. The Muffin had learned what each sound was from Mum and Pops pointing them out to her. She had even gotten to see the coyotes a couple of times. They looked like a breed of dog she had never seen before.

Muffin was listening to the cacophony of sounds

made by the owls and coyotes when she saw lights coming up the gravel road and then turn in at the gate to park. Mum and Pops with bobbing flashlights came walking down the lane each carrying four water jugs and a plastic bag of toiletries. Coming inside the RV, Mum and Pops turned on the dim battery powered lights before putting away the water and toiletries. Muffin getting a good look at them realized they both looked and felt better. Thank goodness!. Sitting down around the table Mum and Pops told Muffin the visit with Sue and Ross was fun and they felt much better after showering. Mum cheered, "We're clean again!" Pops told The Muffin the lane was getting too squishy to pull the Jeep down.

Muffin had been watching them both very intently. No more scratching, that's good. Mum and Pops' eyes were still kind of red but better. "Nope, don't think they have the fleas. Sure am glad about that." She thought, "Whew!"

Crawling into bed that night after covering Muffin with a blanket, Mum and Pops fell into a deep sleep. Mum came suddenly awake at 5am. It was very dark out and there was what appeared to be a spotlight being waved around in all directions. The light's beam even shone into the RV at times. "What in the world?" Mum murmured.

She woke Pops to tell him and they noticed that the spotlight was now up by the gate. The Jeep was parked up there! Mum and Pops both scrambled out of bed, taking turns dressing in the dark so as not to alert whoever was using the spotlight. This made it even more challenging than usual. Mum got as far out of the way for Pops as was possible in the small confines of the RV.

Muffin who had also been woke with all of the commotion had jumped down from the bed thinking it was time to get up. She was standing between them in the dark wondering why they didn't turn a light on. That's when she seen the spotlight up the lane by the Jeep just inside the gate. "Whoa! Let me at em'! Muffin meowed, "I'll teach them not to bother our Jeep!"

Pops who had finished dressing first said he would walk up with no light to see what was going on. Mum dressing frantically told him to be careful she'd be outside in a minute and would bring the phone too. Muffin really wanted to go with them, but Mum wouldn't let her for fear she would get lost in the darkness.

Stepping out of the RV she seen Pops walking past the big Cedar tree and up the lane. All the light now seemed to be focused on the Jeep. Mum began walking up the lane and was about half-way to the Cedar tree when she heard Pops talking to someone. Then the spotlight disappeared before a car started up then drove off down the road.

Mum could see Pops walking back down the lane towards her. "Whew! What happened?" She asked.

"It was a cop out patrolling the area looking for stolen vehicles. Guess there's been someone stealing cars around here. In the darkness he couldn't tell anyone lived here." Pops answered.

Mum laughed, "And with the way we've been having to back up fast to make it inside the gate, the Jeep is covered in mud and usually parked crooked too."

"Yep." Pops chuckled, "Plus he couldn't see the barn cabin or the RV in the dark."

"Mystery solved!" Mum yawned, "Let's go back to bed. Brrr." So back to bed Muffin, Mum and Pops went after their very early morning excitement! zzz...

They were all a little stiff the next morning, so it

took them slightly longer to get around. Mum fixed biscuits and gravy with ham for breakfast. Muffin liked the ham! Afterwards Mum and Pops dressed in layers for barn cabin work. Then letting Muffin back in from her outdoor romp, they gave her a pat before going to work.

Today Mum and Pops would be putting up wafer board on the walls of what would be the kitchen and bathroom. They set up to cut the wafer board inside, having decided it made more work doing it outside. Besides the wind was pretty cold and it was misting! Brr. They would just have to do a daily clean up of the mess.

"Hey," Mum called, "We should bring Muffin over on our noon break."

"Good idea!" Pops smiled.

Mum's sister Sue called to let them know there would be a couple of really cold nights this week. " Supposed to be 10 to 12 degrees. Come and spend the night with us if you want. "Bring Muffin along too!" She invited.

Mum thanked her for letting them know and for the offer. "Wonder how cold the RV will get?" Mum mused.

Pops had begun measuring walls to see how the wafer board would fall out and if they needed any 2x4's. "Well at least we don't have to wire the place. That will save some money." Pops enthused.

Mum nodding in agreement said, "That's right.

Leaves us more money to finish out the barn cabin!"

Adding a few 2x4's where needed, they cut the first piece of wafer board to size. It took Mum and Pops a bit to get that first piece just where it was needed. It had to be right so that the rest would be on the north wall. Without a heat source the barn cabin was very cold. They most definitely had to keep moving!

A couple of hours later the north wall was done. Mum and Pops decided to take a break and go hang out with The Muffin. The inside of the RV was much warmer than the barn cabin. Although by most people's standards the RV would not have been considered warm at all. Muffin who had been lying in front of the kitty heater was mildly startled when Mum and Pops opened the RV door to come in. She was happy for their company! They always snuggled her and covered her with a blanket so that she stayed extra good and warm. Putting the kettle on for hot drinks, Mum and Pops sat down with The Muffin. Petting and talking to her, Pops also doled out a few treats. Stirring up some hot chocolate Mum and Pops snuggled with The Muffin so they could all keep warm together. With their hot drinks finished, Mum made a cold trek to the woods, the wind was blowing and it was misting as well.

Coming back inside the RV afterwards, she warmed herself while Pops covered Muffin with a blanket. "See you later," They told her. Vincent texted letting Mum and Pops know about the extreme cold temperatures for a couple of nights this week. Saying to come on down and stay with him if they wanted. Pops thanked him for the weather report and the offer.

Then walking back over to the barn cabin, they began measuring and cutting wafer board for the east wall. They were only doing half the wall. The rest of it would be done in tongue and groove pine car-siding thankfully. The wafer board was heavy and hard to keep in place. Mum and Pops also discovered that the battery powered skill saw didn't like cutting wafer board. It ran the battery down very quickly. They hoped to get the walls done before the battery died! Pops had already decided not to use the battery powered screw gun much in case he needed to take the battery off of it for the skill saw. He thought with using the bare minimum of screws to put it up, they might be able to get the wafer board cut for the walls.

Becky called while they were working to warn Mum and Pops of the extra cold nights coming up and to be careful. Mum thanked her for the weather update. "Starting to think these cold nights are really going to happen." exclaimed Pops, "Whew!"

The sky was still overcast and misting too, which made it very hard to see inside the barn cabin. Mum shone a flashlight as Pops cut wafer board. They were using the large stack of wafer board like a table to cut on. Mum would stand on top of a piece of wafer board as Pops cut it to keep it from moving. So picture Pops trying to cut wafer board with a battery powered skill saw while Mum is standing on top of the big stack of wafer board. While she is also trying to shine a flashlight so he can see to cut it! Carpentry without electricity is very different! There's no whamming something up in a hurry. Everything just takes longer. With the east wall finally finished, Mum and Pops headed over to the RV to eat their midday meal. Muffin rubbed against their legs as they updated her on the barn cabin. Pops said, "We will show you after we eat and have caffeine!" She was excited to see their progress.

So after their meal the three of them walked over to the barn cabin. Pops scooped Muffin up in his arms to carry her inside. Looking around Muffin could see that Mum and Pops had all but the cathedral ceiling insulated. She also saw some wafer board on the walls. There was also still a huge pile of it stacked on the floor. She couldn't imagine how Mum and Pops would put the insulation on the tall part of the ceiling. If only they had claws to help with that! One thing Muffin did know was that Mum and Pops would find a way, of this she had no doubt.

She suddenly realized that the barn cabin floor was very cold. With her paws still damp from the walk over she was beginning to feel pretty cold. Mum noticing Muffin lifting first one paw then another off the floor realized her feet were cold. Picking her up they went back to the RV and dried her off, then Pops covered Muffin up good with a blanket. She smiled her thanks to them. Although happy to have a tour of the barn cabin, she was very glad to be back inside the RV with its kitty heater! Muffin didn't know how Mum and Pops were managing to work without heat on such cold floors. "They sure are tough." She mused. Working the rest of the afternoon, they got the wafer board hung on the west wall. It was also only half of a wall. After cleaning up, Mum and Pops went back over to the RV, dusting themselves off really good before going inside.

Muffin gave them a welcoming meow! Mum noticing she had been sick wordlessly cleaned it up, making a mental note to give Muffin a more bland diet. Pops sitting down gave her a good rub. "Muffin." He said, "Tonight the three of us are going to have a RV party. We're going to do nothing but snuggle, talk and lounge!"

Muffin and Mum thought that was a marvelous idea. So after toilette, a nice supper and getting dressed in comfy warm layers Mum and Pops mixed some "Muffin Cups". Sitting down they gently rubbed and petted Muffin. She thoroughly enjoyed her kitty massage purring away blissfully! Happy to see her so relaxed Mum and Pops smiled like Cheshire Cats. The three of them tried to take care of each other.

Snuggling together more Mum and Pops talked of old times and new while she listened intently. After a couple of "Muffin Cups", Mum and Pops didn't have quite so many aches and pains either. They left Muffin sleeping comfortably covered up with a blanket when they went off to bed.

Waking up cold around 1pm that night, Mum realized that the RV heater pilot light had gone out. Muffin was looking at her like . "What happened to the kitty heater!" Brr...

Then Mum noticed that the RV windows were white with snow and it was still snowing. She rolled over to wake Pops saying. "I hate to tell you this but the heater's gone out and it's snowing outside!"

They both rolled out of bed. Pops putting on a coat and shoes went to switch out propane bottles in the snow. He came back in shivering with snow in his hair. Pops looked over at Mum holding The Muffin shivering too. Bending down to restart the heater he beckoned, "Come on let's all get back in bed." Mum settled Muffin in between Pops and her at the foot of the bed then covered her with a blanket. Eventually they all became warm enough to sleep.

Rising before dawn the next morning, it seemed brilliantly bright out because of the snow. Putting on a coat, Pops opened the RV door to go outside. Muffin forgetting about the snow leaped out the door after him. She tried valiantly to put the brakes on in midair before landing squarely in the snow. Yikes! With no hesitation whatsoever she sprung right back up into the RV. Mum grabbing a towel began to dry her off. "Poor Muffin." She was saying as Pops came back inside. Muffin rather embarrassed besides being cold was just grateful when Mum sat her down covering her with a warm blanket. Pops lit the oil lamp for light and extra warmth, then filled Muffin's food and water bowls. They all sat together while waiting for the kettle to boil. When it whistled Mum and Pops made their hot drinks.

Eventually it began to feel warmer inside the RV. So giving Muffin a pat, Mum and Pops walked on over to the barn cabin. Muffin having gone bravely out with them while they brushed their teeth, now had decided that was enough snow time for her. So she was in the bedroom alcove nestled in a blanket with the sun shining in on her. Ahh..

Today the plan was to hang wafer board on the kitchen and bathroom ceiling. After deciding how to begin, they then took measurements. Mum stood on top of a piece of wafer board while Pops cut it. The battery was almost ran down by the time he finished. "Well let's see if we have enough battery left to screw this on the ceiling." He said. But first they made a T-bar so that Mum who was kinda short could help hold it up. Otherwise she wouldn't be able to reach the ceiling. Pops could reach up just high enough to screw it in place he thought.

The T-bar made they set it close by, then Mum and Pops lifted and balanced the piece of wafer board. Raising it up as Mum tried to get the T-bar underneath to wedge it in place against the ceiling rafters. There was nothing easy about this. Pops being left to balance and hold the piece alone while Mum struggled to get the T-bar underneath and help wedge it into place. Whew! The first piece was fought with, cussed over and then left to crash to the floor. Luckily without them under it. Pops was cursing and Mum was worried he had hurt himself. Wafer board lifted over head is heavy by the way! Pops had pulled some muscles trying to keep the board from falling on them. So this time they payed more attention to how they lifted and stood when they picked the wafer board up. The second time Mum and Pops set it back down saying they needed to work smarter not harder! The third try they got that sucker screwed into place with just enough battery for the screws needed. Wahoo! Carpenter's dance! "Well." Pops smiled, "Now that we've figured out how to do this, we need to go over to Sue and Ross' to charge batteries."

"Ha ha!" Mum laughed, "Alright I'll go give them a call." Pops gathered the batteries, while she went inside the RV to make her phone call.

" Looking over at Muffin who was now having a snack, She said, "Got to go charge batteries at Sue and Ross' house."

Muffin blinked at her still drowsy as if to say,

"Alright Mum!"

Arriving at Sue and Ross' house, Mum and Pops went right on inside. Ross started the batteries charging while they all had a good visit. Sue had told them to bring empty water jugs too. Later they thanked Sue and Ross, before driving back home. Parking up by the gate since the lane was getting soft, Mum and Pops carried water jugs and batteries down the snowy lane. Putting the water away under the RV sink, they had a snack while hanging out with The Muffin. Pops giving her a couple of treats as well.

Then with a pat for her, they went back over to the barn cabin. With two fully charged batteries they could really get some work done now. Huffing and puffing, while struggling, with an occasional curse thrown in, Mum and Pops managed to get the wafer board hung on the kitchen and bathroom ceiling by around two o' clock. Hungry having not eaten anything since their snack, they decided to go into town for some of that yummy broasted chicken! They let Muffin outdoors while they got ready, although she didn't really like the snow! As Pops brought her back inside the RV Mum sang out, "We will bring you back some broasted chicken Muffin!"

"Did you say chicken?" She sighed, "Ahh chicken!" Mum's brother Scott showed up as they were getting ready for town. He wanted to make sure they knew about the cold weather coming up. Inviting them to come stay at his place if the RV got too cold.

Mum and Pops thanked him for the offer. "This must be going to be some cold!" Mum said.

"Guess we better pick up some supplies while we're in town huh." Pops mused.

Muffin was hanging out on top of the table watching the cows when she seen the red Jeep come up the gravel road, then turn in at the gate and drive down the now frozen lane. She climbed down from the table and waited just inside the RV door, as they got out of the Jeep. Mum and Pops didn't like Muffin on top of the table. So she thought it best that they not see her up there. As Pops opened the RV door Muffin meowed a welcome. She went over to her food bowl so that Mum would know she was ready to eat some chicken.

"O.k. Muffin." Mum smiled, "Let's get you fixed up!" Muffin looked on enjoying the smell of chicken. After eating she walked back over to the door so they would know she wanted out. Pops who was coming back inside after taking supplies over to the barn cabin, let The Muffin out. Leaping out the door she headed over to a nice patch of grass showing through the snow so that she could eat a few greens before exploring. Mum getting a couple of things out of the Jeep noticed Muffin eating some grass. She hoped it would help her tummy. Cats were smart about these things!

By this time it was getting close to dark. Muffin and Mum went back inside together. Water was heated up for washing their hair and taking a sponge bath. Pops who had gone outside to call his Mom came back in saying, "Why don't we go visit Mom and Louis tomorrow? We need a break and they would like some company."

"O.k." Mum replied.

Then filling their yetis with nice warm water they went outside to wash their hair. Chills and shivers! When finished they each took a sponge bath in the tiny RV bathroom. Muffin decided since Mum and Pops were taking their bathes she would too. After supper they all snuggled together for warmth while relaxing. Mum and Pops were still cold from washing their hair outside. Plus the tiny bathroom was pretty frigid too. Sometimes now they had to break ice in the little metal washpan they kept in the bathroom to wash up in! They told Muffin about going to go visit Pops' Mom and Stepdad Louis tomorrow. Then gave The Muffin lots of attention. Rubbing and petting her until she was a very relaxed and happy feline, purring loudly with a half smile on her face. Mum and Pops tired and sore from putting wafer board on the barn cabin ceiling went to bed early that night. Muffin still very relaxed from her rubdown stayed right where she was in the seating alcove! zzz...

Rising early the next morning, Mum and Pops were dressing when Muffin her eyes at half mast struggled to rise. She still felt boneless from the care they had given her the night before. Pops noticing Muffin wasn't very awake yet picked her up and gave her a good petting. Mum put out fresh food and water for The Muffin. Then she put the kettle on to heat up water before she stepped outside to answer the call of nature. Pops went out as Mum came back inside. She set out their cups and caffeine supplies. Then sitting down at the table with a dim battery powered light and a small mirror, Mum attempted to apply some makeup to her face. She decided foundation was as far as she could go in the faint light. Muffin never quite understood exactly what Mum was trying to accomplish when she done this, but she sure got a kick out of watching her. Jolly good entertainment! He he...

They got around quickly and were ready to go in a flash. While the Jeep warmed up they gave extra attention to The Muffin also telling her they would be back before dark that evening. Muffin with all this rubbing and petting was in a very relaxed state. So after watching them drive away, she decided to carry on with the zen-like spa theme. She first ate a light breakfast from the buffet of lovely treats and snacks Mum had left for her. By then it was getting light outside. "Ahh...." Muffin purred, "What a day this is going to be!"

Jumping up into the bedroom alcove she got herself comfortable. Now it was time for birdwatching, a most zen-like thing to do. Especially with the sun shining on the snow and casting lovely rays of light where she lay on the bed. The sun shining in on Muffin warmed her up immensely. Colorful birds flew this way and that way. Between the sun and the beautiful birds she couldn't imagine a better way to enjoy the day. Plus the snow was melting! Birdwatching and napping with a midday break to dine upon the wonderful array of food. Muffin couldn't hardly believe it when she saw the red Jeep coming up the lane. "Wow!" She sighed, "That was some zen-like trance I was in." It had truly been a lovely spa day!

Mum and Pops came inside carrying a few bags. One of which had in it new treats for The Muffin. They pet her a bit then opened the RV door so she could go outdoors. Muffin thought getting some fresh air was the best way to end her spa day and the snow was mostly gone now. Mum and Pops came back outside to stroll around with her, telling Muffin that they had a nice visit with Pops' Mom and Stepdad.

Later they three had a simple meal together then snuggled and relaxed. This was the first evening that it was supposed to be really cold. Mum and Pops had decided to stay in the RV and see how things went. With "Muffin Cups" in hand the three of them covered up with a blanket. In the dim oil lamp light they talked of times in the past when they were kids and the weather had gotten bitter cold. Even remembering times when Becky and Vincent were little and the winter had been extra cold. They checked the outside temperature a couple of times, then decided to stop opening the RV door to conserve heat.

By the time Muffin, Mum and Pops went to bed that night it was 43 degrees inside the RV and was very clear and starry outside. Mum and Pops were both wearing several layers of clothes. Mum was even wearing a stocking cap and gloves! They all got into the bed, Mum and Pops settled under layers of blankets. Muffin was lying on the top blanket covered with one nice warm blanket, since she didn't like too much weight on her. It was toasty warm in bed.

Waking up in the middle of the night Mum checked the inside RV temperature. Brr! It was 32 degrees. Making sure the tiny heater was still on and that The Muffin was covered with a blanket, Mum then covered her head up and went back to sleep.

Around daylight Pops checked the inside RV temperature again. It was 20 degrees! Yikes. The three of them stayed in bed covered with blankets until the sun began to shine into the RV windows. Then leaping out of bed Pops turned on the gas cookstove to heat up water for caffeine, while Mum lit the oil lamp. The cookstove and oil lamp doubled as extra heating sources in the bitter cold. Muffin's water was frozen so Mum got the ice out of it. Quickly eating her breakfast Muffin then jumped up to lie between Mum and Pops. With all of them covered in blankets it was slightly better. But it was then that they discovered that the heater and gas cookstove wouldn't work together in the bitter cold. They had been trying to heat up water on the cookstove, then suddenly realized the burner had gone out. Pops also noticed the heater had quit working too! Whoa. He went outside to investigate. Coming back inside for a fireplace lighter he said. "The gas has frozen up at the regulator. Need to try and unthaw it." Mum followed him out to help and after a time it finally unthawed. Going back inside, Pops said, "Think we're going to have to use one thing at a time. Let's heat up some water, then turn the heater back on." Meanwhile they got back under the blankets with the ever watchful Muffin. For she had been observing their craftiness and was becoming more and more impressed by Mum and Pops' skillful way of handling all of these situations. It was very Warrior like. Yah!

That day was all about trying to keep warm. With the three of them snuggling together for warmth, doing word-finds and reading a little. Trips to the woods to answer the call of nature were very quick trips indeed! Sue called to make sure they were alright, saying it had gotten down to 8 degrees last night! The high for that day was 20 degrees. Vincent, Sue and Scott all told Mum and Pops to come stay with them if they changed their minds. But the three of them being pretty stubborn stuck it out in the RV. The second night was about the same as the first with the inside morning temperature once again at 20 degrees. It was another day of hanging out together inside. Thankfully the sun shone once more. The outside temperature that morning was a balmy 12 degrees and it eventually rose to about freezing at 32 degrees. Wahoo! When Muffin, Mum and Pops went to bed that evening they were happy knowing that the bitter cold snap was over and they could get back to normal again. Or least ways their new kind of normal. He he...

The following morning they were up early. With having had a break for a couple of days Mum and Pops felt they were ready for the task of laying wafer board on the floor of the south loft, this loft needing more floor support. So after hot drinks, breakfast and Muffin duties, they put on warm layers before going over to the barn cabin to begin work. While she with the morning spread out in front of her had decided to lie in the sun and watch the wildlife mill about!

Climbing the ladder up to the south loft, Mum and Pops took measurements before going back down again to cut the first piece of wafer board. Once cut Mum and Pops each got on a side and hoisted it up into the loft. Today was all about weight bearing cardio and of course some stair master! As luck would have it three sheets didn't need cut which really saved the battery on the skill saw. So after hefting the wafer board up into the loft, Mum and Pops grabbed the screw gun and screws, plus some nails and a hammer. Climbing up into the south loft, they screwed and then nailed them into place. Being careful on the low sides of the loft that they didn't whack their heads on the ceiling!

A couple of times Mum and Pops went over to the RV to warm up with The Muffin. With the weather being colder, the inside of the barn cabin was most certainly colder as well. Brr... Sometimes Muffin would go outside to roam a bit when they came over.

By the time noon rolled around they were finished with the south loft floor. The batteries had both died so they would now have to go charge them at Sue and Ross' again. Such was the irony of the situation. Mum and Pops were using battery powered tools since they didn't have electricity, but battery powered tools required electricity to charge the batteries! There was no such thing as getting lots of work done fast. Between charging batteries, short winter days and dealing with the cold inside the barn cabin, they had come to realize that everything just took longer this way. The south loft might be what they got done today.

Mum called Sue about charging batteries. To which Sue said of course. So after enjoying their midday meal together topped off with a cup of joe, much petting was given to The Muffin, before they were off to go charge batteries.

Coming back a couple of hours later, Mum and Pops went outdoors with The Muffin. They strolled happily about together, she sniffed around the old well while they kept a good eye on her. They all walked up to check the mail and on the way back down the lane they hung out underneath the huge Cedar tree. Then Mum and Pops took Muffin inside the barn cabin so that she could see their progress. By then it was late afternoon and all were ready to go back inside the RV to warm up. Evening rituals were finished, then they sat together covered with a blanket for extra warmth. Mum and Pops done a few word finds which made Muffin happy, since she considered this to be good entertainment. So all three were quite content.

The following days were busy. There was the rest of the screws and nails to be put in all the wafer board that was up. At the table inside the RV Pops done some figuring for the pine car siding. They were thinking of covering a large part of the inside of the barn cabin with pine. So Pops wanted to get a price quote on it. Muffin always enjoyed hanging out with Pops while he scratched around on paper. Cat smiles!

Mum's brother Scott came by one evening bringing a rainwater catchment tank with him and they had a good visit. Later when Scott was taking his leave Mum and Pops thanked him again for the tank.

That evening as Muffin, Mum and Pops were eating supper, Vincent texted saying that he could come up tomorrow for a visit if they would like the company. Mum who been reading his text out loud said, "Muffin do you want Vincent to come visit us tomorrow?"

Muffin who was eating her supper perked right up. She gave Mum and Pops the eye as if to say, "Of course I do!" So they made plans for Vincent's upcoming visit. Hoping they would be able to get down to see Becky and her family soon too.

Muffin, Mum and Pops slept in until 7:30am the next morning. All three of them crawled out of bed still a bit groggy. Pops who had stepped outside to answer the call of nature said, "Must be out of gas, the heater's not on." as he came back in.

"That explains why I can't get the cookstove to turn on." Mum yawned.

Turning, he went back outside to put on a new propane bottle. This done, heat was restored and Mum could put the kettle on. Thank goodness! Pops freshened up Muffin's food bowls, then Mum and him sat down to wait for the water to get hot. Soon the much needed cups of caffeine were ready to drink. They sat around the table drinking from their cups in the oil lamp light. Muffin had decided to take a good bath this morning. She wanted to look her best for Vincent. Mum and Pops were planning to go to town and pick up something tasty for their meal.

So properly caffeinated, they loaded the Jeep with the empty propane bottle, water jugs, library books they needed to return and laundry. Then warming up the Jeep, Mum and Pops gave The Muffin a pat. Be back in a couple of hours they said before driving away. Muffin climbed up onto the table to watch the cows for awhile as she took her bath. Much later she jumped down and padded over to lie in front of the heater. Deciding to take a nap before Mum and Pops came home. zzz...

The RV door awoke Muffin with a start. "Whoa!" She yawned. "Mum and Pops had snuck in on her. That must have been some Catnap!" Coming fully awake she watched as they carried bags inside the RV. Pops unloaded a new propane bottle and some full water jugs. Mum set aside yummy food that would be for their feast with Vincent. They had about 45 minutes before he would be there so Pops took Muffin outdoors for a romp while Mum tidied the RV. The air felt pretty brisk outside, making the inside of the RV seem warm when they came back in.

Vincent arrived around 12:30pm. Muffin, Mum and Pops could hear his music playing as he drove down the lane. They all stepped out to greet him as he opened his car door. Muffin having jumped out the RV door, walked over to stand beside Vincent as they talked. He scooped her up as they went inside the RV. He petted and talked to Muffin as Mum and Pops got their RV style feast ready. There was much to talk about as they sat down for their meal. Muffin had her food bowls near Vincent. So once finished eating she lay down beside him. They topped off their meal with a cup of caffeine while she let their voices wash over her.

Afterwards Muffin, Vincent, Mum and Pops all walked over to the barn cabin. Vincent wanted to see their progress and he was curious what would be next. He was very surprised at exactly how they were getting the work done. Muffin roamed around the barn cabin noting that the insulation and wafer board pile had went down substantially. They all got cold about the same time and so walking back over to the RV they went inside.

Vincent worried that Muffin, Mum and Pops weren't keeping warm enough. They told him that just like they were learning old ways to get carpentry done, they were also remembering old ways to keep warm. "O.k." said Vincent. "But it's supposed to be even colder next week. If you need to come down and stay with me for a few nights, please do." Mum and Pops thanked him saying they definitely would if they really needed to.

They talked then of other things. Muffin lay beside Vincent as he played them new songs he liked. He even had some funny cat videos to show them. Muffin looked on in disgust. She would never understand why humans thought this was so amusing. Or how those cats could be so stupid! Grr... She did love some of that super chill music Vincent played though. They all really missed music. But Muffin, Mum and Pops knew that Vincent was working on figuring out a solar powered mini stereo for them. He had the brains to make it happen too!

It was getting to be dusk now and Vincent mentioned heading back to Springfield. So Mum and Pops asked if he would like to join them on a trip to visit Becky and family this next Friday. Vincent enthused, "Sounds good to me! I'll drive us down from my apartment." So plans were made for their trip to

Arkansas. Then with hugs all around Vincent got in his car and with a wave drove off towards Springfield. Muffin, Mum and Pops watched until he was out of sight. Then the three of them strolled about in the walnut grove, before going back inside the RV for the evening.

Rising early the following morning, Mum and Pops took turns dressing quickly into work clothes for the day. Brr...it was cold! Muffin having slept in the seating alcove, decided to stay under her blanket until it warmed up more. Mum turned up the tiny heater while Pops lit the oil lamp. Then he put the kettle on the gas cookstove to heat. With all of their RV heating apparatus' on, the inside temperature began to rise. Muffin deciding it was warm enough jumped down to eat some of the breakfast Mum and Pops had fixed for her. She lay down between them afterwards. Her tummy was kinda upset this morning, she would try to eat more later. They gave Muffin a good rubdown while having caffeine, sometimes that helped her. After breakfast Mum and Pops covering The Muffin with a blanket, told her they were going over to work in the barn cabin.

Bundled up in layers Mum and Pops began measuring the north side of the barn cabin floor for wafer board. They then cleared the tools and swept the floor really good. Some of the wafer board would not need to be cut thankfully, which saved precious battery power! They installed as much wafer board on the floor as possible without moving the stack that was still left. Then Mum and Pops took a break to go hang out with The Muffin and warm up. She was coming out of the litter box when they came in, which made them decide to clean her litter box. Muffin wanted outside too while they cleaned her kitty box.

So they let her roam around before bringing her

back in. Then they pet her up good before going back
to work.

Now Mum and Pops had to move the rest of the
wafer board before they could lay anymore on the
floor. So they moved the remainder onto a part of the
floor that was already finished. After pausing to catch
their breath, Mum and Pops began installing wafer
board again. They had made it to the front door of the
barn cabin by noontime and were very hungry. They
would finish the floor after their midday meal. After
eating, the three of them went outside to stretch their
legs and go check the mail.

"Guess we don't have to worry about getting a
light bill!" Smiled Mum as Pops closed the empty
mailbox.

"That's right!" Pops sang out.

Muffin stopped to eat a little green grass on the
way back to the RV, it usually made her feel better.
She was settling down for a Catnap when they went
off to work again. The rest of the wafer board had to
be cut on an angle . Plus some needed cut long ways
too. Battery powered skill saws did not like long cuts.
But Mum and Pops managed to get all of it cut and
enough screws put in the wafer board before both
batteries died. Whew! After crawling around all day
on the floor they were beat. After doing a quick tidying
up, they called it a day. Both dusting off before going
over to the RV.

Muffin who had been waiting just inside the door,
gave Mum and Pops a welcoming meow before
jumping to the ground. This Cat was ready to roam!
Smiling Mum said, "Hi Muffin!"

Pops watching The Muffin sniff about exclaimed
"Tonight let's take sponge bathes and relax with some
RV drinks!"

Muffin glancing over at them realized they looked

pretty sore and tired. "Think I better give Mum and Pops some Cat care tonight." She thought.

She stayed outside until they both had washed their hair, then went back inside with them. While Mum and Pops took their sponge bathes, she gave herself a bath as well. Then Mum heated up some soup while Pops replenished Muffin's bowls.

After their meal Pops sang out, "Time for Muffin cups!" They mixed drinks RV style in their coffee cups. Then everyone sat down together.

"Ahh...let the relaxing begin!" Mum sighed. That was when Muffin went into kitty masseuse mode. She moved from Pops' to Mum's lap kneading and purring, working on relaxing them and loosening up their muscles. They in turn sighed with pleasure, while petting The Muffin. Ahh...Whew! By the time Mum and Pops had a few Muffin cups and their kitty massage, they were feeling very relaxed and boneless. She was looking pretty happy too. Yah for the zen Cat! Too tired to stay awake the three of them went off to bed with Muffin laying at their feet covered in a blanket. zzz...purr...zzz...purr...

Daylight found Muffin, Mum and Pops still in bed. With their eyes at half mast they blinked at the sun coming up in the east. Wow sun! The RV would warm up today. They had not seen any sun for several days and so were very happy!

Getting out of bed Pops said, "Sure am glad we decided to go to town today and order the pine car siding. Maybe Sue and Ross wouldn't mind if we charged batteries too."

"I'll call Sue after we have our caffeine." Mum answered.

Muffin decided to go outside with Pops so that the cold air could help wake her up." Brr.." she shivered, as they went back inside.

Mum had replenished her bowls so she ate her breakfast. Giving Sue a call about an hour later, they agreed to be at their house early afternoon. As Mum and Pops were leaving for town, Pops told Muffin they would bring her back some broasted chicken. "Meow!" She purred.

Muffin was sitting on the ledge near the door when they came back a couple of hours later. Coming inside Pops said, "Whoa I think Muffin is ready for her chicken."

"You're darn right I am!" She meowed.

He pet her while Mum put some on a paper plate. "Muffin deserves chicken after all the wonderful Cat care she gave us." Mum said presenting the plate to her.

They went over to Sue and Ross' after hanging out with The Muffin. Coming back mid afternoon, Pops put a few more screws in the barn cabin floor, then Mum brought Muffin over so she could poke around while they talked about how to get insulation on the cathedral ceiling.

Later as they hung out that evening, Mum and Pops told Muffin tomorrow would be the day they hung insulation on the cathedral ceiling. "Whew!" She worried, "Sure hope Mum and Pops will be alright working up that high on ladders."

Becky called and talked to Mum and Pops for awhile. They talked about their upcoming visit with Vincent to Becky's house. Next Mum texted Vincent to finish planning their trip. Then with a yawn they went off to bed. zzz...

Waking so early that it was still dark, Mum and Pops realized they couldn't see out the east bedroom window! Looking around they noticed that all of the RV windows were somewhat covered in snow.

"Whoa!" Muffin thought blinking sleepily, "That

snow snuck up on us."

"Well." Pops yawned, "Least ways it will help insulate the RV and keep us warmer! Let's get some more sleep."

Waking again at daylight, they took their time getting around, wanting it to be as light as possible for hanging insulation. At least it wasn't very cloudy today just snowy! It had snowed 2 inches. Muffin happily received lots of extra attention. Meow! Finally Pops said. "Well, we better get started."

So off they traipsed through the snow to the barn cabin with Muffin silently wishing them luck. Dressed in thin layers for good movement, Mum and Pops set up the two ladders they would be using to hang insulation. Mum had chosen the ladder Scott had loaned them. She had nicknamed it "The Beast" because it was a fold up ladder that folded out in more ways than you could imagine. Making "The Beast" a bit ungainly but useful. Pops preferred Phillip's eight foot ladder. Mum would be on the low end of the ceiling and Pops on the high side.

Once their ladders were positioned they each climbed up one to get a measurement, which was doable, just not a walk in the park. Then it was climb back down the ladders to cut insulation. Next Mum and Pops each holding an end of the piece of insulation, climbed up their respective ladders. Yikes! Not as easy as it might sound. One always had to remember they were on a ladder when they went to move a little to get the insulation lined up just right. There was a lot of ladder moving in order to hang each piece of insulation. Plus trying to measure every once in a while to make sure it was still the right size. Stapling insulation over one's head while also trying to hold it in place up high on a ladder was more than just a little scary!

Muffin was sitting on the table watching cows when Mum and Pops padded over in the snow to warm up a couple of hours later. "Oh no, they've caught me!" She meowed. Knowing they didn't care for her on the table. She had felt the need to be up high somewhere, since Mum and Pops were working on ladders.

But they didn't really seem to mind Muffin on the table today. Nope. They were just happy to not have fallen off a ladder so far! As Mum and Pops sat down quietly, Muffin trying not to draw too much attention to herself, got down from her perch on the table and lay between them on her blanket. Pops looking over at her asked, "Are you pretending to be on a ladder like us Muffin?" She looked up quickly to find Mum and Pops watching her but they just smiled.

"Well guess I can't put anything over on them!" thought The Muffin.

Mum and Pops decided to go ahead and eat since it was midday, starting work late sort of made them feel a bit behind. But they really needed the extra natural light today. So they enjoyed a meal with Muffin the wild table Cat! He he. Having hot drinks as they pet her, they all went out for a short snowy stroll afterwards, since the wind felt pretty brisk to them. Then making sure Muffin had everything she needed, they headed back over to the barn cabin to do more ladder tricks.

That evening while Muffin, Mum and Pops hung out it began snowing. Pops had mentioned the snow when he came back in from checking their propane supply. It was a light but steady snow, which was still falling when they went off to bed later that evening.

The following morning when they rose 6 inches of snow lay on the ground. Muffin who had been standing by the door with her eyes at half mast, jumped automatically out the door as Pops opened it to go outside. She tried unsuccessfully to put on the brakes, but still landed in the snow. What a rude awakening! Brr. Mum grabbed a towel as Pops handed a snow covered Muffin Cat to her before going back outside. Muffin decided from here on out she was going to look before she leaped.

Mum went outside to take some pictures. She came back inside saying, "It sure is a pretty snow." But it made everything they did outdoors harder. The call of nature trips to the woods were down right frigid. Muffin who didn't like walking around in the snow, had to be carried when they went outside. Brr...

Trekking through the snow doing two more days of ladder tricks with a few harrowing experiences thrown in, Mum and Pops were able to finish putting insulation on the cathedral ceiling. Muffin for her part was found on the table a lot during this period. It was her way of letting Mum and Pops know she was thinking of them while they were climbing around on ladders!

With the ceiling insulation finished and no snow left on the roads, Mum and Pops were only too glad to leave "The Beast" and it's beastly ladder friend behind. A trip with Vincent to Arkansas to visit Becky, Abe and Ambria were just what they needed! Muffin, after seeing Mum and Pops off, settled in for a lovely, peaceful day. Looking forward to wildlife watching, the spa treats they had provided her with and a general poking about in the RV. Yah!

So while they went off to have a much needed getaway with Vincent to visit Becky and her family, Muffin had herself a zen-like spa day. " Ahh!" They all said. Mum and Pops got back from their Arkansas trip late that evening, looking pretty relaxed they sat down with The Muffin. As the three of them hung out, they

JUDE BALES

talked about their trip with Vincent to Becky's house, telling her they planned to go help Becky when the baby was born.

"O.K." She purred in her zen-like trance.

"Muffin." Pops said, "We hate to leave you again tomorrow but we need to go visit my Mom and Louis.

Muffin gave him a calming look as if to say, "That's alright Pops." For she knew they needed a break after working so hard. Besides this gave her more Cat spa time!

So the next morning Muffin, Mum and Pops got around extra early in the dim oil lamp light. It was still pretty cold outside with the snow still being on the ground. After Muffin had eaten a bit of breakfast she lay down on her comfy blanket in the seating alcove. Her tummy had been acting up a lot lately. She planned to take it easy today while Mum and Pops were away. They rubbed and petted The Muffin a while, before Pops went out to start the Jeep.

Saying they would be back late that afternoon, Mum covered her snugly with a blanket. Then they drove off down the gravel road while Muffin feeling extra comfy and warm decided to take a nap. zzz...

Muffin went about her day studying cows and birdwatching. She discovered that the RV seemed a bit warmer with Mum and Pops not coming in and out. Plus it was a beautiful sunny day!. A Cat could really get warm lying in the sunlight. Meow!

Mum and Pops came back late in the afternoon from visiting his Mom and Stepdad. With the sun waning in the west it was getting colder. This meant the lane was firm enough to drive the Jeep down, so they got to park in front of the RV. Coming inside, Mum noticing that Muffin had been sick went about cleaning it up while Pops sat down with The Muffin.

That evening as they hung out together, Mum and

Pops gently rubbed and petted The Muffin. This always made her feel better!

The following morning while Mum and Pops were having breakfast the lumber yard called, asking when to bring out the pine car siding Pops had ordered. He told them to bring it on out. Muffin was napping when Mum and him went out to help unload it a couple of hours later. Coming back inside the RV afterwards to warm up, Mum said, "Sure hope we find a wood stove for the barn cabin soon."

"Me too." replied Pops.

Muffin having woke up when they came in, jumped down to drink some water and try to eat a little. She was embarrassed because she had been sick again while they were outside, even though Mum always took care it without saying a word.

Sitting down Pops sighed saying, "Man I sure am tired today."

Nodding, Mum yawned saying, "I am too. Maybe if we keep moving it will pep us up."

So after giving The Muffin some tender loving care, they headed over to the barn cabin. Tiredly watching them go she hoped they felt better soon. Cutting the plastic from the pine car siding, Mum and Pops began putting it on the east wall of the living room. The pine was really pretty and mildly pepped them up. They had set up to cut the pine outside using the porch like a table to cut off of. Luckily there was freshly charged batteries for the skill saw. Pops was nailing the pine on the walls as they tongue and grooved the joints together. Excited about how fast it was going Mum and Pops finished the east wall all but the last piece. It would need to be cut long ways. They would do long cuts another day to conserve the batteries.

It was 12:30pm by then so Mum and Pops walked

over to check on The Muffin. When Pops opened the door she got up slowly then leaped out of the RV onto the ground. "Muffin seems tired too doesn't she?" said Mum.

"Yes she does." Pops replied concerned, "If she doesn't feel better by in the morning we should take her to the Vet in Osceola."

"I think so." Mum said softly, "She's been getting sick more often lately."

This decided they went outside with Muffin. She roamed around eating certain grasses and exploring. She still liked to try to look under the tin on the old well, very mysterious you know. Squirrels were also running about for Muffin to enjoy.

Cold, they three headed back to the RV with Pops carrying The Muffin. "Guess we should eat something. Maybe some soup? I'm not really hungry are you?" Mum asked Pops.

"Sounds fine to me. I'm not very hungry either." Pops replied.

Muffin who had been feeling the urge to hock up the grass she had eaten suddenly got sick. "Whew!" She sighed, "Sure hope that settles my stomach!" Pops went into action cleaning it up, then he sat Muffin next to him so he could rub and pet her.

This seemed to relax Muffin greatly although she was kind of embarrassed about it all. "That's alright Muffin. You just relax." Mum said. Sitting down after putting the soup in bowls, Pops and her slowly ate. "Feels like I'm in a time warp or something." Mum sighed.

"Maybe caffeine will wake us up." Pops replied. Yawning they drank a cup. Then covering Muffin with a blanket, Mum and Pops went back to work. What was left of the afternoon went quickly. They were moving so slowly that little of the car siding ended up on the west living room wall. With twilight suddenly upon them, Mum and Pops trudged over to the RV to spend the evening with Muffin. Personal toilette was done quickly, Mum decided to wash up Muffin's bowls, before replenishing them with food and water. Then sitting down they had a light supper. Afterwards the three of them covered up with a blanket close together for warmth. With all of them tired and falling asleep, at 7:30pm Muffin, Mum and Pops crept off to bed, hoping to sleep off the tiredness.

Waking up in the middle of the night, Mum's throat felt raw and she was so stuffed up she had trouble breathing through her nose. Getting up to put some Vicks on, she got back in bed hoping to wake up feeling better. Muffin who was sleeping in front of the heater meowed softly to her as Mum got back in bed. Mum was just falling back asleep when Pops and her heard Muffin being sick. Mum got back up long enough to clean it up and pet The Muffin, knowing Muffin would be embarrassed about it. She murmured, "Don't worry about it Muffin. It's alright." Muffin looked up at her silently thanking her. Mum covered her warmly with a blanket in the seating alcove before going back to bed.

SICK DAYS

1st day sick. It was broad daylight before Muffin, Mum and Pops woke up the next morning. Mum had a headache from sinus congestion and her throat was so raw she could hardly talk. Pops had a body ache, headache and his throat was ticklish. Muffin who had been sick again was lying in front of the kitty heater. "Oh poor Muffin!" Mum squeaked getting out of bed to pet her, before she cleaned up the mess. "We'll take you to the Vet later and see if he has something to make you feel better."

Muffin who really didn't like Vets, did think it would be nice if she didn't have to go around hocking her food up all of the time! "I mean really." Muffin thought, "This is getting ridiculous."

Getting around was a very slow process since they all felt crummy. Hot drinks were even more important than usual. Muffin was given her blandest food and lukewarm water. No one ate much of anything. The three of them just sat together not talking trying to feel better. "Guess that's why we were so tired yesterday." Pops yawned, "We had this coming on." Mum nodded her head in agreement.

By 10:30am they felt ready enough for Muffin's 11am Vet appointment, which Pops had managed to get her earlier. As he warmed up the Jeep, Mum put her coat on and got a blanket for Muffin to sit on. Then they all went out to the Jeep. Pops who was carrying The Muffin sat her on Mum's blanket covered lap.

Getting in the driver's side of the Jeep Pops said, "Alright Muffin! Let's go get something for your tummy."

As they drove off down the gravel road Muffin who had been looking out the window thought to herself, "Sounds good to me!" She hadn't rode in the Jeep since they had moved to Roscoe back on December 18th, 2019. Muffin enjoyed looking out the window. This time she knew about the rough gravel roads and wasn't startled by them. This gypsy Cat liked to ride! Once in town a brief stop was made to pick up cold medicine. Then they drove to the Vets.

Getting out of the Jeep Pops came around to the passenger side to take Muffin from Mum's lap. As they went inside Muffin began to have second thoughts. There were strange cats and dogs everywhere! Thank goodness Mum and Pops were there with her. The Vet came out and had them go into another room so he could examine Muffin. After much poking and prodding with a few hisses and growls, he sent her home with a couple of medicines he thought would help. Muffin was feeling mighty cagey by then and was giving the Vet her most imposing glare. "Let's get the heck out of here! " She growled.

Arriving back at the RV, the three of them went

inside. Muffin was groggy but felt a little better. The Vet had given her a dose of medicine before they left. Mum and Pops got The Muffin settled in comfortably, then they each took a dose of daytime cold medicine before going off to work in the barn cabin. They got pine car siding halfway up the west living room wall before the batteries wore out on the skill saw, so plans were made with Sue and Ross to charge batteries. Mum and Pops went over to the RV to check on Muffin, having some of the broasted chicken they had picked up in town while they were at it .

Muffin who had just woke up from her nap blinked at them as they came inside. Smelling something good she remembered, "Oh yeah Mum and Pops picked up chicken." Her tummy didn't feel too bad either. Maybe she would have some of it later! After giving The Muffin a good petting, Pops let her out to roam around under the RV while Mum and him ate. They could tell she wasn't ready to eat yet, but was feeling better.

Pops brought Muffin back inside awhile later for her next dose of medicine. "Yuck!" She meowed, "But at least it seems to be helping."

"Sorry Muffin." Mum sighed, "Know you don't like the medicine." They gave her lots of attention as they drank a cup of caffeine.

Then Mum and Pops drove off to charge batteries at Sue and Ross' house. Mum had made sure they knew that Pops and her had a cold, even saying they would just drop the batteries off and come back later. But Sue and Ross weren't concerned about their cold so Mum and Pops stayed to visit.

Coming back later they stepped inside the RV to see how Muffin was doing. She was up and giving Mum and Pops the eye that clearly stated, "Where's my chicken?" Pops put some on a plate for her which she promptly ate. Yum! She promptly began giving herself a bath in the seating alcove afterwards.

Smiling happily to see her feeling better, Mum and Pops went over to finish the west wall of the barn cabin. As luck would have it they even got a small partition wall between the kitchen and living room covered in pine too!

Once done cleaning up and putting away tools, Mum and Pops walked tiredly over to the RV. Muffin who was hanging out by the RV door when they opened it hopped down to the ground. Time to explore a bit! Mum and Pops fixed supper making sure The Muffin's bowls were well attended to. Stepping back outside Pops scooped up Muffin and brought her inside so they could have supper together. It was a light meal since no one was really hungry. Then it was all about getting comfy. None of them were very with it. Covered up together with blankets, Mum and Pops done word finds as The Muffin watched them in the dim oil lamp light. Finally saying enough was enough the three of them crept off to bed. Mum and Pops each took a dose of cold medicine as they went. Muffin thankfully didn't need any more until morning.

2nd day sick. Morning found Mum and Pops feeling a little worse for wear. Muffin looked to be feeling better though! Mum had developed a bit of a cough, while Pops' body ache was much more noticeable. Getting around was a very slow process, with hot liquids being most important. Muffin ate some breakfast then settled down for a nap in the seating alcove. Pops standing up more from habit than anything else said, "Well, time to get to work." With Mum and him both taking a dose of cold medicine, before giving Muffin medicine too, with a sorry because she didn't think much of it.

It was another low light winter day, cold but not bitter thankfully. Mum and Pops set up to cut car siding outside on the porch again. Then fell into the pattern of measuring and cutting pieces of pine. It was outside to cut, go back in to hang the car siding on the angled south wall of the living room. Having still not found a wood stove yet Mum and Pops were cold inside the barn cabin besides it being pretty cold outside on the porch too.

About halfway through the south wall they took a break to go warm up with Muffin. Mum fixed them some hot chocolate while Pops gave Muffin a little chicken. Yah! Tin arrived for the kitchen walls an hour later. Pops and the delivery guy carried it down from the gravel road. The lane was just too soft for the delivery truck to pull down. Mum and Pops were glad the tin had arrived since the car siding for the downstairs walls was almost gone! After having a midday meal, the three of them walked up to check the mail, stopping at the barn cabin afterwards to show Muffin their progress. She liked to see all the new happenings!.

Going back over to the RV to warm up afterwards, they gave The Muffin a pat. She was getting ready for a nap as they went off to work again.

Watching them walking over to work on the barn cabin, Muffin worried, "Whew! Mum and Pops don't look so good. Maybe the Vet should have gave them some medicine too. It doesn't taste good but my tummy feels better. Think I better keep an eye on them."

Mum and Pops came back over to the RV several hours later, accidentally startling a sleeping Muffin who was in front of the kitty heater. Mum was hacking a lot and Pops was walking oddly saying it hurt to move. "That's it!" Muffin meowed, "It's time for a Cat intervention." Jumping into action Muffin rubbed against Mum and Pops legs purring as she did so. This seemed to have a calming affect on them. After washing up as best as they could in their state of unwellness, supper was then eaten before Mum and Pops sat down for the evening. Muffin the Zen Master kneaded and purred them into a deep state of relaxation. She could tell Mum and Pops felt at least temporarily better. In return they rubbed and petted The Muffin. So benefits were had by all. That night the three slept very well. ZZZ...Cheers for the Zen Master Cat!

3rd day sick. It was broad daylight when they awoke the next day. Muffin could hear Mum and Pops coughing, saying they had a headache and body ache. Mum couldn't hardy breathe through her nose. "Man." Muffin thought, "Good thing we all take care of each other." Slowly they got out of bed. Hot drinks were made as soon as possible. Muffin had been given her breakfast and those oh so cold trips to the woods were made. Brr! Toast was eaten by Mum and Pops before they all took some medicine then Muffin went outside to roam for a bit. She came back inside as Mum and Pops headed off to work in the barn cabin.

They had gotten all of the tin put on the kitchen walls yesterday. Thankfully! Cutting tin with heavy duty scissors is hard on the hands! It really looked good though. They had some accent cedar to hang on the east wall of the kitchen today. The cedar was lightweight and fun to put on the wall, which was nice after working with tin. Vincent texted Mum and Pops while they were on a break with The Muffin. They let Vincent know that they were all sick. But that Muffin had gotten some medicine for her tummy. They tried to discourage him in coming to visit them, worrying he might get sick, but Vincent insisted on coming up to check on them. So plans were made for his visit the following day. Mum and Pops decided they would just have to wash up good and give the RV a good cleaning. Muffin was over the moon about Vincent coming tomorrow. She decided then and there to give herself an extra good bath!

The rest of the day Mum and Pops worked on finishing the cedar accent wall. The lumber yard brought out pine car siding they had ordered early that afternoon. Mum and Pops were outside with The Muffin when they saw the delivery truck coming up the gravel road. Mum scooped up Muffin and put her inside the RV, then went to help Pops and the delivery guy unload the truck. The lane was still too soft for the truck to pull down. So the pine was placed on the ground just inside the gate. With Mum and Pops carrying it the rest of the way down to the barn cabin from there. Whew! Going inside the RV afterwards they gave Muffin a good petting and her medicine. She didn't like it but at least it seemed to help.

Then armed with cough drops and hot drinks, they went back to the barn cabin, both thinking it would be nice to try a few pieces of pine car siding up in the south loft. Climbing up into the loft to take some measurements, they went back down the ladder and out onto the porch to cut the pine, then climbed back up into the south loft to begin. The first row of pine had to be good and straight otherwise the tongue and groove wouldn't go together. Taking care to stagger to the seams for the best over all look, Mum and Pops had trouble with the second row fitting into the groove. Luckily anticipating this Pops hadn't nailed the first row all the way down. So with only a bit of adjustment they were able to get the first two rows tongue and grooved together well. Two more rows were measured and cut with a few minor adjustments made. Then they were finished with the lower east wall of the loft. Saving the very last row which was a long cut for another day.

Feeling pretty worn out Mum and Pops crawled over to the ladder, taking turns going down it while the other held on. They cleaned up the porch, then trudged over to the RV. Muffin daydreaming about their visit with Vincent tomorrow was taken completely by surprise when they stepped inside the RV.

"Clean up and chillaxing tonight Muffin!" Pops coughed. Mum put the kettle on to heat up water to wash their hair and take sponge baths. Watching them both Muffin just didn't know how Mum and Pops did it! They looked like they were sleepwalking. Yet they were still getting so much done. She couldn't believe the amount of work Mum and Pops had done since they had gotten sick. Thank goodness tonight was all about relaxing! So once clean with comfy clothes on, a light supper was had. Then the three of them sat down together snuggled up with a blanket. Muffin was given much petting and in return she purred which always seemed to relax Mum and Pops.

Becky called to see how they were doing. Pops had let her know a couple of days ago that they were sick. They hoped to be well before she had the baby. Her due date was coming up soon. Surely they would be! Later plans were made to thoroughly clean the RV and make a trip to town in the morning before Vincent arrived. Muffin loved it when yummy treats were picked up for their meal with Vincent! Meow! By this time Mum and Pops were starting to look like balloons someone had let the air out of. So taking some cold medicine, the three of them went off to bed with Muffin laying at their feet covered with a blanket. That night Muffin and Pops were kept awake by Mum snoring loudly! No matter what Muffin and Pops done they couldn't seem to wake her up or get her to roll over. Yikes! She sounded like a chainsaw for pete sakes. Whew! That night Mum slept soundly while Muffin and Pops only slept fitfully.

4th day sick. The next morning they woke up around 8am. Mum ask Pops, "Did you sleep good? I sure did."

Pops was like, "Nope."

She replied, "I wonder why?"

Yawning Pops answered, "You snored all night.

Muffin and I couldn't get you to stop." "Dang! Sorry." Mum replied weakly.

As they got out of bed, Mum well rested, Muffin and Pops with eyes at half-mast, much caffeine was drank. Muffin eyeing Mum thought, "I'm having myself a nap when they go to town!"

Mum cleaned the RV after breakfast. Then Pops and her drove off to town leaving Muffin to her Catnap. Zzz... She was still looking a bit groggy when Mum and Pops came walking down the lane and into the RV after their short trip to town. They had been parking just barely inside the gate lately, the lane was still too soft to drive on. Pops bleary eyed unpacked groceries while Mum put them away, keeping out foodstuff for their meal with Vincent. Muffin was happy to see that fish was going to be on the menu! Yum.

About 1pm Vincent drove up the gravel road and parked on the shoulder of the road. Carrying his backpack and a cloth bag he walked down the lane. Muffin, Mum and Pops met him about halfway. "I brought you a care package." Vincent called out. Handing the cloth bag to Pops, he scooped up The Muffin as they all went inside the RV. "Whoa, smells good in here!" He said.

"Fish, Clam chowder and french fries!" Mum replied, as they sat down for their RV style feast. Noticing some tinned smoked oysters in their care package bag she put them on the table as well. Vincent asked how they were doing. He could tell that Mum and Pops weren't feeling the best. They told him they had definitely felt better, but that the medicine the Vet had given Muffin seemed to be helping her. Feeling guilty Mum told Vincent she had kept Muffin and Pops awake last night.

"She sounded like a chainsaw." Pops yawned,

"Muffin and I couldn't figure out how to shut her off!" Half trying not to laugh Vincent said, "Dang!

maybe the supplements I brought will help with that." The wonderful feast was topped off with much needed caffeine. Vincent caught them up on what had been happening down his way. He also showed Mum and Pops the supplements he had thoughtfully brought along and how to use them. "Wow! Look at all these wonderful soups and tins of fish!" Mum

enthused, "Thank you so much!"

"Hey you're welcome!" Vincent smiled, "Glad you like them."

Muffin was rubbing against his leg to thank him for the tins of fish and pouch of cat food he had for her. Vincent scooped up Muffin to pet her as Pops yawning big said, "We can use them that's for sure. We cleaned up extra good in hopes that you don't get any of this."

"I'm sure I'll be alright." Vincent smiled.

Everyone went outside to walk around in the walnut grove. Mum's brother Scott showed up to visit and to check out the barn cabin progress. Vincent who hadn't seen his Uncle Scott for awhile was very happy to see him. They all went inside the barn cabin so Vincent and Scott could see what Mum and Pops had been up to. Mum made sure Scott knew they had a bad cold and not to get too close to them. There was talk about the different things Mum and Pops had accomplished in the barn cabin. Plus Vincent and Scott got caught up on what was happening in each of their lives. Muffin prowled about looking the barn cabin over. Every once in awhile she would walk over and stand near Vincent as he visited with everyone.

Needing to get back home, Scott said his goodbyes and walked on back up the lane to his truck. By then Muffin, Vincent, Mum and Pops were cold and so went back inside the RV to warm up. "Sure hope you can find a wood stove for the barn cabin soon." Vincent said.

"We do too." Pops replied.

They all talked about their ideas for the non-electric barn cabin. Lots of interesting thoughts were shared. Muffin lay contently up against Vincent purring happily. She loved having days like these! All three of her favorite humans together in one place. Vincent asked how The Muffin was doing. Though she had lost some weight he had seen that she was eating. Mum and Pops told him that the medicine seemed to be helping her tummy. Hopefully when it ran out Muffin would still feel good. "She even ate some broasted chicken the other day!" Pops said. Vincent upon hearing this gave The Muffin a pat on the head. In return she gave him one of her famous Cat smiles!

Seeing the light was fading outside he said better head back to Springfield. So they all walked up the lane together with Vincent holding The Muffin. Giving her a kiss on the head as he handed her to Pops he said. "I'll see you next time Muffin!" Then saying he hoped they all got to feeling better soon, Muffin, Vincent, Mum and Pops gave each other a group hug.

"Text us when you get back home." Mum called

out.

"O.K. will do." Vincent replied. He drove off down the gravel road, with Muffin, Mum and Pops waving before walking back down the lane.

That evening after Vincent had texted saying he had made it back home, they all went to bed hoping to sleep well. What really happened though was that Mum snored like a chainsaw again, with Muffin and Pops sleeping fitfully in between bouts of trying to get Mum to either wake up or roll over. Yikes! She sounded terrible plus she was so loud. It was another long sleepless night for Muffin and Pops.

5th day sick. The next morning Mum had only to get a look at The Muffin and Pops to realize that neither had gotten much sleep. "Oh no! Sorry!" Mum rasped. This cold had really settled in her throat. Muffin and Pops just gave her a bleary-eyed stare, too tired to say anything. Mum got up and put the kettle on to heat, then she lit the oil lamp and fixed up Muffin's food bowls. This gave them a little time to have a lie in. Mum felt it was the least that she could do considering she had kept them both awake two nights in a row.

By the time Muffin and Pops dragged themselves out of bed Mum had all the morning chores completed. So that all they had to do was sit down at the table. Whew! Pops drank his coffee while still in his sweatpants with his hair standing on end. Muffin just lay on her blanket staring off into space with a distant look in her eyes dreaming of sleep. Mum was trying to be as quiet as possible so as not to draw attention to herself and to make up for all the noise she had made during the night. Yikes!

Both Mum and Pops had a body ache, headache, sinus congestion, sore and itchy throats and coughs. They were taking daytime cold medicine, so that they could continue working in the barn cabin. Muffin still had some medicine left too, which seemed to be helping her tummy. Plus Vincent had brought Mum and Pops some great supplements! They both took these while Muffin ate the new cat food Vincent had brought her. After three cups of coffee Pops declared himself ready to go to work. Muffin perked up hearing this, knowing that soon now she could have an uninterrupted nap!

So Mum and Pops headed off to work in the barn cabin, both dressed in layers for warmth. The sun was shining a bit. Yah! Muffin seeing the sunlight on the bed climbed up into the alcove to lay in the suns warmth. Ahh. Just what a sleep deprived Cat needed. She spent the morning napping and watching the birds and squirrels. She had been seeing a bird that Mum and Pops called a woodpecker lately. Muffin had been trying to figure out how they pecked on the trees like they did. They done it with such speed and intensity! It made Muffin's head hurt just thinking of it. "That's it!" She thought, "I'm watching those funny squirrels for awhile." She found them much more relaxing. So relaxing in fact she fell asleep, dreaming of squirrels doing somersaults while swinging from limbs in the trees. Zzz... purr... zzz...

As Muffin slept, Mum and Pops began the process of setting up, measuring, cutting and then bringing the pine car siding up into the south loft, continuing where they left off a couple of days ago. Neither Mum or Pops were really fit for working, their colds were pretty severe. Although Mum had been sleeping the last few nights she really didn't feel any more rested than Muffin and Pops. But they just went right on putting car siding on the south loft ceiling, half delirious never even considering not working on the barn cabin. They climbed up and down the ladder, hunching and crawling this way and that way under the low ceiling trying to get the pieces of pine tongue and grooved together. Sometimes they simply had to sit down on the loft floor to rest from all of their efforts.

With one half of the ceiling done, Mum and Pops climbed down from the south loft. Both batteries had died and they were thinking of checking on The Muffin, plus getting something to eat. Mum also had arranged for Pops and her to go get batteries charged at Sue and Ross' house. As they came inside the RV, Muffin jumped down from the bedroom alcove looking more rested from her nap on the sunlit bed.

Mum heated up some soup while Pops pet The Muffin and gave her some treats. While eating they got a text from Vincent saying he had woke up not feeling the best and so had taken the day off work.

"Dang it!" Mum exclaimed, texting Vincent that they hoped he felt better soon, to take it easy and rest. "Hope he has some medicine and supplements he

can take." Pops worried.

Muffin who had stopped eating upon hearing that Vincent was sick, tried to send good vibes out to him so that he would feel better. They were all pretty bummed that Vincent was sick and hoped he would get well soon. Mum and Pops gave Muffin her medicine before going over to Sue and Ross' to charge batteries. They visited awhile since Sue and Ross didn't seem to mind that they had a cold. After the batteries were charged it was back to work again in the south loft.

The rest of the afternoon Mum and Pops worked. By the time they ran out out of light to see, they almost had all the car siding up in the south loft. With only the middle seam trim left to do! Exhausted, Mum and Pops climbed safely back down the ladder. After cleaning up the front porch work area, they stumbled back over to the RV, brushing each others clothes off outside before going in.

Muffin was just stepping out of her litter box as Mum and Pops came inside the RV. Looking over at them she did a double take. Whoa! They weren't really talking they were just mumbling to her and themselves. Mum and Pops were kind of moving, but like in slow motion. Muffin had never seen anything like it before. Luckily they didn't seem to want to do anything more than heat water up in the kettle to wash up and make hot drinks. Muffin was afraid of what might happen if they tried to do more than heat up a kettle of water. Pops managed to replenish Muffin's bowls. Mum just sit out random things that didn't require cooking for Pops and her to eat.

They sat there eating crackers and cheese and crackers and butter, all the while petting The Muffin. As she eyed them worriedly, Mum and Pops staggered back up realizing they hadn't changed into comfy clothes yet. Changing clothes became quite an affair since Mum and Pops in their delirium were both trying to change clothes at the same time! Muffin thought they were going to knock each other out a couple of times. Both of them flailing around in the tiny confines of the RV like that! She was very relieved when Mum and Pops finished changing. But then opening the RV door they both went outside to brush their teeth! Muffin jumped out the door after them, thinking she had better keep an eye on Mum and Pops. About the time they looked like they were done brushing their teeth, Muffin started meowing loudly by the RV door. Thankfully this got Mum and Pops to open the door for her. Teeth chattering they decided to come back inside with The Muffin.

It was dark outside by then and the coyotes were

howling. The three of them all sat down, Mum and Pops were shivering under the blankets they shared with The Muffin. Chills from their sickness made them feel even colder than normal. With wintertime in an old RV and an unheated barn cabin already being pretty damn cold. Nothing was really said and Muffin almost would have thought they were asleep if Mum and Pops' eyes hadn't been open.

Rousting himself Pops mumbled, "I think we should just go to bed."

Nodding Mum murmured, "I think so."

Muffin watched as they went about with much effort getting ready for bed. Medicine was taken and Vicks put on, then Mum and Pops crawled into bed with Muffin following to lie at their feet. Mum pet her then covered her up with a blanket. All of them then fell into a very deep sleep. Zzzzzz...

That night all three slept without waking until broad daylight. They blinked their eyes in the bright light. None of them felt like getting up, so rolling over Muffin, Mum and Pops went back to sleep again.

6th day sick. Two hours later they lay in bed half an hour before deciding to get up. With stuffy noses and a bad cough Mum and Pops heated up water for caffeine. Muffin slowly climbed down from the bed to make her way to the litter box. Mum freshened her food bowls then took turns with Pops going to the woods to answer the call of nature. Fixing hot drinks, they sat down at the table with Muffin. Mum and Pops kept trying to roust themselves to get ready for work on the barn cabin, but no matter how much they tried it just wasn't happening. Studying them, Muffin could see that she would have company today inside the RV. "At least I won't have to worry about Mum and Pops on ladders!" She sighed, "Whew!"

Mum did text Vincent. He was feeling a little

better but had taken off work because of a bad cough. "Sounds like Vincent is getting over this cold quicker than we are." Pops mused. Muffin was very happy to hear this! Becky called to see how everyone was. Mum and Pops told her that The Muffin was doing pretty good, but that they were still struggling to get over this crazy cold. But with any luck at all they would be well before the baby was born.

Then gathering books and word finds Mum and Pops settled in to hang out with Muffin. Although Mum and Pops thought they might eventually feel like working, what really happened was that they sat around all that day with The Muffin. She stayed right with them too, trying to be moral support if nothing else. They did go outside a couple of times, thinking the fresh air might revive them. Mum and Pops just flat didn't have any energy, trying in their delirium to work while sick had exhausted them. Pops went outside once to call his Mom. Muffin and Mum worried that he might not make it back to the RV afterwards. Considering how out of it they were it was a possibility. They were very relieved when Pops finally dragged himself back inside shivering.

The rest of the day passed with Mum and Pops having some lucid moments. Muffin never left their sides. Even though Mum and Pops didn't eat much of anything that day, they made sure Muffin had everything she needed. They were still taking medicine for their multi-symptom colds. Muffin on the other hand had finished taking all of her medicine yesterday. Mum's sister Sue called to see how they were doing. Mum just told her they were feeling pretty tired today. After a day of trying to read and do word finds, with Muffin as their faithful companion, the three went quietly off to bed hoping to wake up feeling better in the morning.

7th day sick. Daylight found them all waking up cold! Mum and Pops both got up to go outside and hook up a new propane bottle, then coming back inside to restart the heater. Brr...still wore out and shivering with cold they got back in bed with The Muffin. Making sure she was covered up with a blanket, Mum and Pops went back to sleep.

At 9am, once more awake they lay there in a daze. After a time, they got up thinking it might make them feel better. But after having hot drinks with still no improvement, Mum and Pops had to admit that they would not be working today either. Feeling lucky to each make it to the woods and back without mishap, Mum filled Muffin's bowls for her, then Pops and her sat down.

Feeling totally drained they spent the day not really talking, petting Muffin every once in a while. Pops kept trying to read but kept falling asleep instead. Mum just sat staring vacantly off into space, she might have slept, she wasn't sure. Muffin would get up to have a snack and walk around a bit or use her litter box, but then she would lay back down again between Mum and Pops.

By the end of the day, Pops muttered, "We've really got to try not to do this tomorrow!"

In total agreement Mum answered, "I know. This is some weird kind of bug we've got!"

Muffin was very relieved to see them rallying.

"Thank goodness!" She sighed.

The three of them went to bed early again that night. Mum and Pops gave The Muffin a good petting in appreciation of her sticking with them in their hour of need. What a Cat! Stars glittering they all fell asleep.

8th day sick. So the next morning even though Mum and Pops didn't exactly feel full of energy, they got out of bed at daylight. And along with The Muffin ate breakfast after having drank their cup of joe. Then taking turns making trips to the woods to answer the call of nature, Mum and Pops gave The Muffin a good rubbing and petting. She seemed kinda out of it this morning. They figured Muffin just needed some extra rest, after all she had been taking care of them for two days now. Mum and Pops were going to make sure she got all the rest she needed plus all the spoiling too!

Checking to make sure The Muffin had everything she could possibly need, they walked over to see how best to get started in the barn cabin. Having finished all but the middle trim seam on the ceiling in the south loft, it meant they would now have to work off of ladders again to put car siding up on the open cathedral ceiling. More pine car siding would be delivered this morning thankfully, since Mum and Pops were just about to run out of it.

Though still feeling pretty rough, Mum and Pops had a tiny bit of energy today. Slowly they cleared the area where the ladders needed to be for hanging car siding. Ladders in place they each gingerly climbed up one. Mum on "The Beast" and Pops on Phillip's 8 foot step ladder. Both trying to not fall off a ladder while still getting a good measurement for cutting the car siding. It was a scary and tedious process, with Mum and Pops working on autopilot.

Both knowing they just wanted to get the barn cabin finished and get a wood stove put in it so that Muffin and them could live in a warm place. This was something that was constantly on their minds. The driving force that kept them moving even while they were sick, with the cold as their companion inside the unheated barn cabin.

As Muffin watched Mum and Pops go off to work in the barn cabin, she hoped they would be alright.

She knew that neither one of them were in very good shape. Mum and Pops were pushing on in spite of it all so that the three of them could move into the barn cabin as soon as possible. Muffin knew they would locate a wood stove too. Mum and Pops were very good at finding the things that they all needed. Waking up in the middle of the night last night, Muffin had discovered that her tummy didn't feel right again. She decided then and there that she was going to be extra careful of what and how much she ate. Muffin also planned to eat some grass the next time she went outside. Maybe she had just eaten too much the day before. Muffin determined that some Cat spa days were just what she needed. Birdwatching, napping, bathing and eating lightly were just the things to get herself in tip top shape again! Meow...

Car siding was delivered midmorning and as luck would have it the truck carrying the pine was able to pull down near the barn cabin. Mum and Pops were very relieved, knowing that they just didn't have it in them to pack car siding down the lane on foot. Whew! After unloading the pine into the barn cabin, Mum and Pops took a break in the RV. The Muffin they were happy to see was having a Cat spa day. Before heading back to work they took her out for fresh air, noting that she ate some grass as they did so.

With Mum and Pops steadily hanging pine car siding the rest of the day, they managed to get half of the open cathedral ceiling done. This with only taking a break to eat at noon and one short afternoon break! Both times Mum and Pops brought The Muffin outdoors to stroll about. She was sick once outside when they had their late afternoon stroll. But Mum and Pops thought that was because Muffin had eaten too much grass. Happy to have gotten half the cathedral ceiling done without any ladder mishaps, they straightened up the barn cabin and slowly walked back to the RV.

Having decided to wash up good tonight, Mum and Pops brushed off their clothes and began heating water up for taking sponge bathes and washing their hair. Muffin greeted them at the door, then jumped to the ground to go sniff about under the RV. Coyotes were already beginning to howl as Mum came outside to wash her hair while Muffin explored. Pops came outside next. He began washing his hair as Mum went inside to sponge bathe. Muffin came back in with Pops just as she was done bathing. Then it was soup with cheese and crackers for Mum and Pops. With them setting out what appeared to be Muffin's most desired Cat spa foods. Feeling exhausted but pretty accomplished, they three spent a short but lovely evening together too tired to stay awake for very long. Zzz...

9th day sick. The following day after morning rituals were completed, Mum and Pops went over to begin hanging car siding on the other half of the cathedral ceiling, their main objective was to try to finish this side of the ceiling. Hoping to do so safely and not run out of energy before it was done. Though clean from their bath the evening before, they still felt pretty lousy and zombie like. They had been in their sick daze for so long, that Mum and Pops had almost forgotten what it felt like to be well. But they refused to do anymore sitting around in the RV days. No can do they said! Not if we're going to get the barn cabin finished for Muffin and us to move into.

Muffin, after getting Mum and Pops off to work began her Cat spa day with watching those funny squirrels! She napped afterwards until Mum and Pops came over for a short midmorning break. Then she walked around outside looking at all of the puffy clouds in the sky. As they went back to work, The Muffin gave herself a good bath. She was nibbling a little of her Cat spa food when Mum and Pops came in for their midday meal. Muffin strolled outdoors with them for awhile afterwards. Then she spent some time studying the cows. Later after a nap feeling an overwhelming urge to be sick, Muffin jumped down from her blanket to the floor before doing so. Drat it! She hated when she made a mess Mum and Pops had to clean up.

Elated that they had gotten the other half of the cathedral ceiling done, Mum and Pops walked back over to the RV. Muffin was sleeping in front of the heater when they opened the door to come in. Giving Mum and Pops an "I'm sorry." look Muffin jumped out the door to go exploring.

Mum noticing she had been sick began cleaning it up. "Dang it!" She said, "I thought the Vet said the medicine he gave Muffin would help her."

"No." Pops sighed, "He said he hoped it would help."

"I guess that was probably so." Mum answered softly, "But if the three of us have anything to do with it she will get better!"

"I know that's right." Pops said, "Don't forget about Vincent too. He will be researching ways to help The Muffin!"

The discussion ended, Mum and Pops went outside to hang out with Muffin. They had been very relieved to hear from Vincent a couple of days ago that he was over his sickness. With any luck at all Muffin, Mum and Pops would be well soon too. Walking back to the RV, Muffin mused, "We three need to get well so Vincent can come see us!"

They spent the evening in the dim oil lamp light,

Mum and Pops trying to read and doing word finds, with The Muffin lazily watching them. Then off to bed with Muffin deciding to sleep right where she was in the seating alcove. Owls were hooting and they could hear foxes yipping and howling as they drifted off to sleep.

10th day sick. The next morning the sun shone and it seemed warmer. Yah! Muffin having been ill the night before, jumped out the RV door as soon as it was opened. She thought the sunlight would be good for her. It also gave Mum and Pops room to clean up her dratted mess. Coming back inside afterwards, she heard Mum and Pops talking about going over to Sue and Ross' house to charge batteries this morning. So they three had a light breakfast, after Mum and Pops were properly caffeinated. Then they drove off down the road for battery charging duty.

Feeling better Muffin was just settling down to birdwatch in the bedroom alcove, when just on the other side of the big Cedar tree, she seen four deer. Whoa! Muffin really enjoyed watching the deer. For a long time they just meandered about flicking their short little tails. They were almost to the south fence line inside the Walnut grove, when Mum and Pops came driving up the gravel road in the Jeep. Then as Muffin looked on, the deer, their tails flipping up and down wildly, turned back to the north, the direction from which they had came. Leaping into action the four springy footed beast bolted and then jumped the north fence effortlessly before running off into the woods. "Bravo!" Muffin enthused, Deer never failed to inspire her with their grace and beauty.

Mum and Pops having no idea that they had helped create such an entertaining event for The Muffin, came inside the RV to see how she was doing. Muffin from her spot on the bed gave them a beaming

Cat smile in appreciation of their part in the deer's performance!

"Boy, Muffin sure is in a good mood this morning." Pops commented.

"She sure is!" Mum replied. Cat smiles...

Having begun the day with charging batteries and now getting a late start on the barn cabin, Mum and Pops decided they would just have to see how much work they could get done today. First to reset up since they would now be hanging car siding in the north loft. Getting a ladder in place they climbed up to take measurements and begin the process once more to tongue and groove the pine together.

Noontime came quickly with only a few pieces of pine being added to the north loft. Cold and hungry Mum and Pops walked back to the RV. Muffin greeted them with a "Meow" as they came inside. Pops picked her up and began petting her while Mum fixed them all something to eat. Then after having some hot drinks, the three went outside to stroll about in the sunshine. Pops decided he better move the Jeep up by the gate since the lane was getting soft. It was nice in the sunlight so they stayed outside longer than usual.

Then Muffin went off to have a nap in the RV while Mum and Pops worked in the barn cabin. Becky called as they were cutting a piece of pine. So Mum and Pops talked to her for awhile. Becky seemed to be doing well. They hated to tell her they still weren't feeling the best. Telling her they were working hard on getting over this confounded cold, wanting to be there when the baby was born. Sue had even offered to keep an eye on Muffin when the time came. Now if they could just get well!

After their phone conversation with Becky, Mum and Pops got back to work putting up pine. They were beginning to discover that it was becoming more difficult to tongue and groove the car siding together. 36 feet is a very long row indeed and what the length of the cathedral ceiling happened to be. They pushed on for a couple of hours, stopping at 4pm because it was just getting too hard to see in the north loft.

Having succeeded in getting a little more than half of one side of the north loft ceiling done they decided to call it a day. Now it was Muffin time! She was waiting for them just inside the RV door as Mum and Pops came in. Bounding out the door she looked around determined to find another type of grass. She had been quite ill while they had been off working in the barn cabin. It must be a different grass that was good for tummy trouble. By the time Muffin came back inside the RV she was kinda tired, but she had found another grass to try though. Mum and Pops having cleaned up the mess while she was out, now planned to be Muffin's Cat slaves that evening.

So after supper they took turns gently rubbing and petting her. Careful not to rub too hard. She wasn't purring as much as normal but this did seem to relax her. As Mum and Pops went to bed that night they covered The Muffin up with a blanket right where she lay, because she was fast asleep! Zzz...

11th day sick. Rising at dawn Mum and Pops first checked on Muffin. She was sitting in the front of the heater giving them the "Let me out" look.

So they opened the door to let her out. Still hacking with stuffy noses Mum and Pops surveyed the floor to see if Muffin had been sick. Only once it looked like, their rubbing and petting must have helped. Yah! As she came back in a little while later Mum and Pops told The Muffin that they had to go to town for supplies. It was pretty cold outside today but the sun was shining beautifully. So after the three finished their morning rituals they made sure The

Muffin had everything she needed before driving off to town.

Muffin who had settled down on top of the table at their departure, was just beginning her bath while waiting for the cows to appear in the field out of the south window. She looked outside every so often as she bathed. Glancing out the window at one point with her right back leg hiked up in the air as she was washing it, Muffin's sharp eyes seen what looked like two dogs at first glance in the farthest field to the south. But upon closer inspection The Muffin recognized them to be coyotes! She really admired their thick red brown fur. As she watched the two began frolicking as if in some sort of coyote game. Muffin was mesmerized as she watched the two at play. It was like they were putting on a show just for her!

Then one coyote began chasing the other around. Suddenly within touching distance of it, the one in hot pursuit of the other, jumped and landing on top of the other coyote tackled it to the ground! The two coyotes rolled around on the ground wrestling wildly. "Whoa!" enthused Muffin, "This is some kind of show!" They were scuffling around with dust and fur flying as if one of them might be named a winner in this wrestling event. Muffin was totally involved with this scene and almost ready to place her own bet on who the winner would be even. It was then with no warning that the two shaggy coyotes jumped up and both frolicking again ran east through the field. They crossed the gravel road and continued on east leaping and pouncing around like a couple of kids. Muffin watched the two coyotes until they were out of sight. "Ahh...such grand entertainment!" She meowed, "He he."

Getting back late morning Mum and Pops having

eaten broasted chicken in town had brought some back for The Muffin. Parking the Jeep just inside the gate since the lane was mushy, they came down the lane towards the RV carrying clean laundry, screws, nails and grocery bags. They let Muffin outside right away. Then after putting everything away, they stepped back outside to walk around with her. Muffin, who was still thinking of the two coyotes began her own frolicking about playing Cat games. Mum and Pops joined in scurrying this way and that way with her, laughing when The Muffin flung herself on the ground and started rolling around. They were happy to see her having so much fun! Playing with The Muffin was always high on Mum and Pops list of priorities. The three went back to the RV smiling. Meows and Cat dances...

After giving Muffin a bit of the broasted chicken, Mum and Pops headed over to the barn cabin. With working the rest of day they managed to finish one side of the cathedral ceiling in the north loft. Feeling lucky that even with this confounded nasty cold, that they were able to just push thru and keep on working without falling off a ladder! With darkness soon approaching, they tidied up and walked over to the RV. It was Muffin time now! So after a brief clean up Mum and Pops sat down to their meal with her.

Vincent was going to call this evening and they were excited to hear from him. So when the phone rang later on everyone sat down together to await their turn to chat with him. Pops talked with him first asking how things were going in Springfield. Next he put the phone up to Muffin's ear so that Vincent could talk to her. Muffin really enjoyed this, she didn't understand how it worked but she would recognize Vincent's voice anywhere! She would purr and meow now and then so that he would know that she was listening to him.

Then Mum took her turn updating Vincent on how everyone was doing. She also made sure he was still healthy. Mum told Vincent that even though Muffin wasn't feeling very well that she just kept on going forward as best as she could. "I think Muffin is a true warrior just like in those Warrior Cat books you used to read." Mum said, "She inspires Pops and I to get over there and work in the barn cabin even when we don't really feel like it."

Vincent totally agreed saying, "I think Muffin might just be the Greatest Warrior Cat of them all!"

"Did you hear that Muffin?" She exclaimed.

Muffin looked up questioningly, "What? What is it?" Smiling Mum put the phone down to Muffin's ear just as Vincent's voice came through the phone saying, "Muffin you're a Warrior! I think you just might be the Greatest Warrior Cat of them all!"

Muffin hearing this sat up straighter and smiling she "Meowed" her love and thanks to Vincent into the phone.

Picking up the phone Pops relayed Muffin's reaction to her being a Warrior Cat to Vincent. I love you's were said all around as Muffin the Warrior Cat sat up at attention strong and proud. She had always believed Vincent saw her for the wild Warrior Cat that she was and was happy that Mum and Pops believed she was as well. Purrs...Smiles...Warrior Cat dances...

When the three went off to bed later that night, Muffin decided to sleep in the seating alcove. Mum and Pops were still coughing, sneezing and sometimes snoring. Muffin thought the seating alcove might be a better place to be until they were feeling better. A little easier for a Cat to sleep this way.

THE GREATEST WARRIOR
CAT OF THEM ALL

A s she drifted off to sleep on a magic carpet ride of Warrior Cat proportions, Muffin dreamed of going into battle with enemy cat warriors. In her dreams Muffin the Greatest Warrior Cat of them all and her beloved Vincent stood tall together battling those enemy cat warriors. Vincent just like in her previous dreams was covered in fur and had claws like a cat instead of fingernails. In unison Muffin and Vincent with fangs bared charged, letting out deafening growls and roars. Running head long at the enemy with such wild untamed determined force that the enemy cat warriors with terror in their eyes turned tail and ran. Muffin and Vincent shook clinched paws at the backs of the enemy cat warriors. Then letting out glorious "Meows" they did Cat dances of victory!

Muffin came awake with a start realizing that her legs were moving like she had been running. It was the middle of the night and the stars were glittering.

She looked around the RV to see if Vincent was curled up in a corner somewhere or doing Cat dances by the door. Her Warrior Cat dream with Vincent in it had been so real. Who was to say that it wasn't? Exhausted from Vincent and hers' battle with the enemy cat warriors, Muffin fell into a supremely happy and deep sleep. Zzz...purr...

12th day sick. Everything from that moment on became like a gossamer dream. Muffin, Mum and Pops might have be very ill, but nothing or nobody could break their resolve to be the best they could be for one another. Mum and Pops learned more of The Muffin's Warrior Cat ways too. They became even more fierce about getting the barn cabin done. Friends and family who came by to check on their progress were amazed by how much work they were getting done without electricity. Muffin, Mum and Pops just shrugged it off, too delirious to really comprehend what they had accomplished. Themselves and everyone else never realizing just how sick they were.

Muffin, Mum and Pops had become very good at rising at first light and going about their day working until there wasn't much daylight left. That's what you did when you didn't have electricity. Oil lamps and battery powered lights were what they had for lighting when it was too dark to see inside. Hauling water from Mum's ole home place had become second nature. As had washing one's hair outside in the cold or walking to the woods in the rain to answer the call of nature. In a very short time Muffin, Mum and Pops had crossed a line that none of them had seen coming. There was no knowing if the three would ever be able to get electricity or a well for running water due to the easement issues. Even if they were able to Muffin, Mum and Pops had crossed the line already and in doing so would never be the same again.

In these days of their gossamer dreamlike trance Muffin, Mum and Pops moved more freely and felt as though they could see more clearly than ever before. Muffin would go outdoors and become one with the landscape, stalking birds and rabbits even, seeing how close she could get to them. She became so good at this that Mum and Pops thought she just might catch one if she should decide to. Muffin and the squirrels became sparring partners out under the Walnut trees. The squirrels would bark and talk to her, in return Muffin meowed and sometimes let out fierce growls. They ran this way and that way after each other as if in a great battle.

When Muffin and the squirrels' sparring games eventually ended Mum and Pops would cheer. "Yah Muffin the Greatest Warrior Cat of them all!" They sang out. Then as she came back over to them, Mum or Pops would scoop her up petting Muffin as she purred loudly!

A day became more endless to the three, with Muffin, Mum and Pops noticing the richness that each moment held in it. Every once in awhile time even stood still for them. They were companions of the highest kind. Vincent called often and talked to Muffin, Mum and Pops. He was their fourth companion, who even from a distance had tapped into the gossamer dream world that they were living in. He then drank from their cup of otherworldliness, crossing over to the edge of Muffin, Mum and Pops' separate reality. Vincent standing tall with them, the four Warrior like companions shimmering in the golden haze...

GOSSAMER DREAM WORLD

Nothing could have prepared the four companions for the journey in which they would take. Or of the way in which Muffin, Vincent, Mum and Pops would travel there. Having heard of the gossamer dream in low murmurs from a scant few who had the inner vision and knowledge of how to enter into the gossamer dream world thru the golden haze, the four companions prepared for their journey. Giving much thought to which possessions and their worthiness for travel with them. Once chosen these items were put in small packs to be carried upon Muffin, Vincent, Mum and Pops' back. They then told select family and friends of their plan. Best wishes were spoken and the four companions smiled light hearted, happy knowing their loved ones understood the four of them's need to make this journey into the gossamer dream world. Lining up beside each other, Muffin, then Vincent, then Mum, and then Pops walked together towards the shimmering golden haze. The four companions stood in front of it with their backs to home and loved ones. Each raised a hand in acknowledgement to everyone. Then with wondrous shouts of pure joy the four companions ran together as one into the golden haze...

Muffin, Vincent, Mum and Pops were enthralled by the golden haze and its beauty. This time traveler's trip of otherworldly proportion was a dream come true. They each began to experience a freedom of mind and body that none had felt before. There was an exuberance in all of the four companions conversations. They soon realized that the golden haze was beginning to thin out and that they were catching glimpses of the gossamer dream world. Muffin, Vincent, Mum and Pops looked on in awe, transformed by what they seen.

As the four companions emerged fully into the gossamer dream world from the shimmering golden haze, they were enchanted by how lustrous and ancient the gossamer dream world was. Joyous grins spread over Muffin, Vincent, Mum and Pops' faces. With eyes wide with wonder they set off on an epic journey!

For wild gypsies they became with wanderlust in their hearts and a song upon their lips... Moving freely together as one, Muffin, Vincent, Mum and Pops breathed in air as sweet as nectar and feasted upon the bounties of the land. There were times in their travels the four companions would come across enemy cat warriors who would eye them with evil intent and advance upon them to do battle. It was then that Muffin, Vincent, Mum and Pops would turn into the true Warrior Cats that they were. Moving with such agility and swiftness that they were on top of the enemy cat warriors before they knew what had hit them. With great roars and growls Muffin the Greatest Warrior Cat of them all and her three Warrior Cat companions fought and then drove the enemy cat warriors away limping as they went.

Evenings became magical to these wild gypsies. For in their travels of far away lands the four companions found wonderful hidden enchanted places to camp of the evening. Muffin, Vincent, Mum and Pops would sit around the campfire boisterously recounting tales of their battles with enemy cat warriors. They would all let out wild yowls that would set the wolves, coyotes and foxes to howling.

Then as the campfire died down the four companions would gaze upon the multitude of stars in the sky. There were conversations about the vastness of the universe and how all was one. Thoughts were shared of the ancient peoples from the past and of those who had yet to come into this world. For they were only waiting for their time to come forward to be. Then Muffin, Vincent, Mum and Pops reminisced about old times together, laughing at some of the funny things they had done. As one the four would rise to rekindle the fire with a mystical meditative glow in their eyes. Then as the campfire began to burn more brightly the wild gypsy companions would dance with great abandon around the fire together, in honor of one and all...All is one...

Each day Muffin, Vincent, Mum and Pops arose excitedly, with all eager to discover what great adventures it held for them. For their journey together was glorious! They were amazed by just how long a day could be in this other worldly gossamer dream that the four were living in. In their travels they came across other gypsies of their kind roaming the land whom the four companions had lively conversations with. Sometimes Muffin, Vincent, Mum and Pops would camp a few days with these gypsies. Campfires would be prepared and food for a feast would be gathered. Music would be played and there was much dancing around the campfire. Then as the fire died down there would be storytelling amongst the four companions and their gypsy friends, with toasts being made in peace, goodwill and happiness...

With each day feeling like a lifetime, Muffin, Vincent, Mum and Pops became known far and wide. For distance was no barrier to them with time seeming so endless. In living this gossamer dream life without bounds, the four gypsy companions saw many a rare and beautiful thing. Such that are only visible to those with inner vision and the outer sense of sight that goes along with it.

Now and again the four companions came across enemy cat warriors who would throw down the gauntlet, challenging them to battle. It was in these times that Muffin, Vincent, Mum and Pops would turn into the fierce Warrior Cats they had become known to be. Their growls and deafening roars unnerved the enemy cat warriors even before the four Warrior Cat companions began to do battle with them. With Muffin the Greatest Warrior Cat of them all always leading Vincent, Mum and Pops into battle with the enemy cat warriors.

The four Warrior Cat companions became renowned for their skills in battle. So much so that any and all enemy cat warriors would challenge Muffin the Greatest Warrior Cat of them all and her three Warrior Cats to battle. Hoping to best the four Warrior Cat companions and thus be considered superior to them in battle. These enemy cat warriors were looking for fame for the wrong reasons. For they were evil, greedy cat warriors who sometimes had even been cast from their own villages. They were no match for Muffin, Vincent, Mum and Pops, so had to flee in defeat, their tails between their legs. The four Warrior Cat companions would then stand tall together, watching the enemy cat warriors flee as they shimmered in the golden haze...

Muffin, Vincent, Mum and Pops were held in very high regard by all they became known to in their journeys of the gossamer dream world. With the enemy cat warriors being the only exception, for they hoped to gain enough power so as to obtain all their greedy minds wanted. These four true Warrior Cat companions in their victory over the enemy cat warriors in battle had protected their fellow man from them and their evil ways. Muffin, Vincent, Mum and Pops were beloved by many for this. So whenever it was known of enemy cats in an area the Warrior Cat companions were traveling through, the four were alerted.

It was a time of much goodwill amongst the people in the villages the Warrior Cat companions came across in their wanderings. Sometimes when Muffin, Vincent, Mum and Pops were going through a village, they were asked if they could stay so that the villagers could hold a feast in their honor. The four Warrior Cats always joined in the hunt for wild game and plant foraging for these events, wanting to make sure there was plenty to eat by all. For they treasured the kindness of these lovely people in the gossamer dream world. The four companions wanted to make sure the villagers knew how much they appreciated them. These celebration feasts were wonderful carefree times! Many games were played, there was dancing to lively music and stories told as well. Lasting friendships were made at such gatherings.

There came a time when Muffin, Vincent, Mum and Pops knew they should go back to their homeland. As much as the four loved this gossamer dream life that they were living, there was no way for them to know how family and friends were back home. For in this separate reality they were unable to contact their loved ones.

So it was decided, that the four companions should make their way back home. All who heard the news were saddened to be losing the company of the four Warrior Cat companions who had become such wonderful friends to them, though they completely understood the need to be with family and friends. The night before Muffin, Vincent, Mum and Pops were to begin their journey back home, the village they were near had a celebration feast in the four companions honor. There was much regalia worn and a merry time was had by all! The celebration went deep into the night, with many a toast being made for happiness and health.

THE GOLDEN HAZE

The following morning Muffin, Vincent, Mum and Pops were preparing to be on their way. Everyone in the village came out to see them set off on their journey home, there were handshakes, hugs and much cheering. As the four Warrior Cat companions took their leave of the village golden haze shimmered in their wake...

This seemed to set the tone for Muffin, Vincent, Mum and Pops' way in which they would make their trip back to their homelands. As the four Warrior Cat companions went through villages in their travels, folks would come outside to cheer for them and sometimes give them food for their journey home. It seemed a runner had been sent ahead of the four companions so that all would know and be able to see them off on their way. This was done in a quiet way so as not to alert the enemy cat warriors. Muffin, Vincent, Mum and Pops were overwhelmed by everyone's generosity.

In their travels the four Warrior Cat companions were still sometimes challenged by the enemy cat warriors they came across. With Muffin the Greatest Warrior Cat of them all and her three Warrior Cat companions rising up as one, their fierce battle cries unnerved the enemy cat warriors. With their all as one fighting skills overpowering the enemy almost before they could begin to fight. Then as the enemy retreated the four Warrior Cat companions would let out loud roaring Meows and do Cat dances!

A strange or maybe not so strange thing happened as Muffin, Vincent, Mum and Pops were making their journey home. For it seemed that as they began a new days travel to their homelands, all that was left behind from only the day before would lie shimmering in a golden haze behind them. As if all of the wonderful adventures with friendly gypsies and villagers besides enemy cat warriors had never been. And yet the four Companions knew with a certainty that all of this was real. Muffin, Vincent, Mum and Pops had made lasting friendships and each had a few momentos from their wanderings far and wide. Besides they all had the odd bite or scratch mark from enemy cat warriors. So the four Companions learned to love with even more intensity this gossamer dream world. Realizing anew that it would all disappear when the four of them returned to their home and family.

But there were still seemingly endless days in Muffin, Vincent, Mum and Pops journey homeward. Just the four of them being together on this time traveler's trip alone made it a grand adventure! For this gossamer dream world had brought the four companions even closer together than ever. Their journey went on in much the same manner, with villages cheering for the four Warrior Cat companions as they made their way through. Sometimes they even stayed for a night in a village when weary from their travels. The villagers always fed Muffin, Vincent, Mum and Pops well, knowing that the road to their homeland was long...

Suddenly there began to be reoccurring stories from the people in the villages and friendly gypsies that the four companions met along the way home. It seemed that the enemy cat warriors were joining together in larger bands with the intent of ambushing the four Warrior Cat companions before they made their way back home. The enemy cat warriors did not want Muffin, Vincent, Mum and Pops to leave this gossamer dream world before they were defeated and victory was theirs.

So the four Warrior Cat companions became even more silent and cautious. They were like ghosts in the forest. Even wild game was sometimes surprised by them as they silently passed through the forest. The villagers had also become more quiet about the four companions. People no longer cheering, but shaking hands and giving hugs to Muffin, Vincent, Mum and Pops as they traveled through their villages. Conversations were now had in whispers when the four Warrior Cats talked with people along the way. It was beginning to appear like there might be at least one if not more who sympathized with the enemy cat warriors. For someone seemed to be alerting these enlarged bands of enemy cat warriors of the whereabouts of the four Warrior Cat companions, with Muffin, Vincent, Mum and Pops trying to avoid a run in with the enemy cat warriors who's numbers had rose greatly!

As the four companions got closer to their homelands, time began to speed up and spiral until it slowly became more like how the passage of time was in their homeland. Muffin, Vincent, Mum and Pops were within a couple of days now of passing through the shimmering golden haze of this separate reality and returning back home to their loved ones. The villagers and friendly gypsies were doing their best to help the four Warrior Cat companions stay clear of the enlarged bands of enemy cat warriors. Muffin, Vincent, Mum and Pops were so close now that tomorrow they should be back home again. They looked forward to seeing their family and friends again! They also knew that when they crossed over into their homeland that the enemy cat warriors would not be able to follow them. For all those who had tried had failed and no one knew why. It appeared that those who had always lived in the gossamer dream with one day the length of a lifetime, were unable to handle the speed up of time in the unaltered world from which the four companions had come. Thus they would perish upon trying.

Bedding down that night to rest before the last day of their journey home; Muffin, Vincent, Mum and Pops were thankful that by late tomorrow afternoon they would be back home again. They were camped on the outskirts of a village, who's people had promised to help keep watch so that the four Warrior Cat companions could get some sleep before the last day of their journey home. All seemed quiet until two hours before dawn when a guard from the village came to warn Muffin, Vincent, Mum and Pops that the band of enemy cat warriors were near.

So the four Warrior Cat companions rose quickly and made their way through what would be the last village on their journey home. Many friends were there to see them off. One friend pulled Muffin, Vincent, Mum and Pops aside telling them that it was thought that the runner who had been alerting the villagers of when the four Warrior Cat companions were near their village was thought to be a traitor. This runner had also been disclosing their whereabouts to the enemy cat warriors. The villagers were outraged by this betrayal! Muffin, Vincent, Mum and Pops thanked their friends in the village profusely, saying that it was very much appreciated and would not be forgotten.

Bidding farewell to their many friends, the four companions made haste moving with as much speed as possible. For they still hoped to stay ahead of the large band of enemy cat warriors. They wanted to avoid a battle if they were able to because they were severely out numbered. So the four Warrior Cat companions last day in this gossamer dream world had an urgency to it that none of them had bargained for. The four were very much hoping to arrive back in their homelands before encountering the enemy cat warriors.

They knew for certain that crossing back over into their homelands would not be a problem, for the four Warrior Cat companions had heard it whispered of back home. There were those who had gone forth into the gossamer dream world and had also come back again through the golden haze to their homelands.

Muffin, Vincent, Mum and Pops managed to stay clear of the enemy cat warriors all that day, each of them very surprised by this. The four companions were walking through a meadow looking carefully around when in unison they spotted the shimmering golden haze just past some huge ancient Walnut trees that were off in the distance. The four began to smile relieved and happy knowing this was where they would cross over to go home.

It was at this moment that out from behind some Walnut trees only halfway across the meadow stepped the enemy cat warriors. So many of them too. Muffin,

Vincent, Mum and Pops looked at one another knowing what they would have to do, with everything they had ever wanted to say to one another shining in their eyes. The enemy cat warriors were slowly advancing towards the four companions. Amongst them was the village runner who was no doubt now the traitor. The large band of enemy cat warriors threw down the gauntlet in a challenge to the four companions. Knowing this was the only way they would ever make it home, Muffin, Vincent, Mum and Pops eyes now glowing with a deep intensity transformed themselves into the true Warrior Cats that they were.

Their growls and roars could be heard for miles. Even from their homelands through the golden haze family and friends turned their heads listening thinking they heard thunder. Not realizing the sounds were coming from the gossamer dream world. The enemy cat warrior band let out growls and roars of their own emboldened by their sheer numbers against the four Warrior Cats. Muffin the Greatest Warrior Cat of them all and her three Warrior Cat companions then rose up as one to rush the enemy cat warriors. But hearing something from behind them they quickly glanced back. The sight that they were met with made their jaws drop!

For there standing were all of the friends they had ever made from the many different villages the four companions had been through in this gossamer dream world. Some of their gypsy friends were there as well. This show of support was more than Muffin, Vincent, Mum and Pops could ever have imagined. For it was apparent that their village and gypsy friends intended to join in on the battle. There were smiles of friendship and gratitude all around.

When the four Warrior Cat companions turned

back to face the enormous band of enemy cat warriors, the enemy cat warriors eyes showed their shock at this turn of events. But they were not going to back down from their challenge. This band of enemy cat warriors felt they had nothing to lose and so were steadfast in their decision, even if it did mean fighting villagers and gypsies as well. Seeing their decision in their eyes Muffin the Greatest Warrior Cat of them all let out a deafening roar before leading not only her three Warrior Cat companions, but villagers and gypsies into battle! The enemy cat warriors rose up to meet them still believing that victory would be theirs.

The two sides came together with much force. Muffin who was in the lead hit her opponent so hard that it sent him airborne landing in a heap on top of half a dozen of his fellow cat warriors knocking them to the ground. Then it was tooth and nail fighting with the enemy cat warriors band trying to push the four Warrior Cat companions back away from the golden haze, which was their only way back home. The villagers were slowly beginning to surround the enemy cats on three sides. Which meant the only direction they were able to go was backwards towards the golden haze. This was something the enemy cat warriors had not expected. Thinking they would only be fighting Muffin and her three Warrior Cats and thus would be able to surround them in a circle and fight to the bitter end. No the enemy cat warriors did not like this at all. For they knew that if they themselves ended up in the golden haze, they would perish.

So while Muffin the Greatest Warrior Cat of them all, her three Warrior Cats and the gypsies were waging an amazing battle against the enemy. The enemy cat warriors were struggling just to remain in the fray with them, instead of being pushed into the golden haze by the villagers and die without even having been in the battle. It was complete mayhem with Muffin the Greatest Warrior Cat of them all and her troops gaining ground on their enemy!

With the battle now taking place in amongst the huge ancient Walnut trees with the golden haze just behind, the back line of enemy cat warriors were now all but touching the golden haze. As the villagers began closing the gap, this back line of enemy cat warriors became frantic. They literally began hurling themselves over the top of their fellow cat warriors away from the golden haze and thus into the heart of the battle. Some however were pushed completely into the golden haze perishing immediately. There were a few of the enemy cat warriors who hurled themselves into such heavy battle that they died before they hit the ground. Confusion became rampant with the front line enemy cat warriors sometimes killing one of their own by mistake.

Muffin the greatest Warrior Cat of them all, her three Warrior Cats and the gypsies were also beginning to show signs of the battle. Though still fighting vigilantly they were tiring from this long extended fight. They knew if something didn't happen soon that the enemy cat warriors would most certainly keep them from ever making it back home again. The villagers had now driven all but two rows of enemy cat warriors into the golden haze. Though a few still continued to escape the golden haze by hurling themselves back into battle.

Muffin, who had been wounded in the torso was still fighting as if nothing had happened. Vincent, blood running down the side of his face from a nasty gash deflected an enemy cat warrior like he was a piece of fluff. Mum, who had been knocked down hard by an enemy cat sprang back up, unable to use her left arm. Snarling in fury she began fighting with only her right arm as if that's the way she always did it. Pops, almost dragging his right leg rammed into an enemy cat warrior so hard he flew up off the ground backwards, screaming into the golden haze. The gypsies had taken to flinging enemy cat warrior opponents into the golden haze whenever possible, thus eliminating them from the battle.

An interesting thing began to happen as the numbers on the enemy's side thinned down to about the same as the four Warrior Cats and their gypsy friends. The remaining enemy cat warriors began nodding their heads smiling. Then calling out to Muffin and her Warrior Cat companions saying, "This has been a magnificent battle! Would that we all live another day to challenge one another." Muffin the Greatest Warrior Cat of them all and her three Warrior Cats upon hearing this and seeing the admiration in the enemy cat warriors eyes, nodded also saying, "Would that this be true. We could come again another day and challenge each other to a more friendly competition in battle!" The enemy cats then shouted, "Let this be so!" The villagers and gypsy friends had been listening to this exchange and had noticed that all seemed sincere in this agreement to call an end to the battle. "But will you allow the four Warrior Cat companions to go home?" demanded the villagers and gypsies. The enemy cat warriors answered this by saying, "Yes as we ourselves would like to return home to our families. So we would like to see Muffin the Greatest Warrior Cat of them all and her three Warrior Cat companions return to theirs'."

So all at once instead of fighting each other in battle, the four Warrior Cat companions and the now not so enemy cat warriors began shaking hands and talking all at once curious about one another. The villagers and gypsies joined in on the conversation too. Much relief was felt by everyone, and in this place they were standing among these huge ancient Walnut trees with the golden haze behind them, was a fitting place for this alliance to occur. These huge ancient Walnut trees held so much wisdom in them that the four Warrior Cats and the other cat warriors chose their words more carefully trying to make the most of their time together before Muffin and her three companions went back thru the golden haze to their homeland.

With the time approaching when Muffin, Vincent, Mum and Pops would be going home, the villagers, gypsies and new cat warrior friends gathered around to see them off. It was at that moment as they four were walking towards the golden haze that Vincent, Mum and Pops saw that Muffin was weaving on her feet a bit due to a wound in her torso. Just as they were moving closer to help her, out from behind one of the huge ancient Walnut trees jumped the traitorous runner. Muffin the Greatest Warrior Cat of them all who was closest saw him first. The traitorous runner had a spear and was moving with much speed towards her. Although slightly disoriented and in pain Muffin rose up to do battle with him, but moving too slow the runner speared her in the torso before she was able to move out of the way.

Mortally wounded now, Muffin the Greatest Warrior Cat of them all, as if in a trance went head long into battle with the traitorous runner. But for all the blood coming from her torso those who witnessed this were in awe by Muffin's grace in battle. She had even sent Vincent, Mum and Pops the eye shouting, "Let me have him!" All those who were present, the villagers, gypsies and new cat warrior friends were transfixed by this sudden turn of events. The runner met Muffin in battle confident of being the winner. But in one fell swoop Muffin the Greatest Warrior Cat of them all, moving with amazing swiftness for one so wounded, snatched the spear from the runner's hands. Then swinging it around with the point aimed at him, her eyes glowing she threw the spear with much force and speed back at the runner, thus disposing of him.

Cheers went up from the villagers, gypsies and new cat warrior friends. Vincent, Mum and Pops ran forward towards Muffin who upon victory had turned and taken a bow to acknowledge their cheers for her. Vincent, Mum and Pops realized then the extent of Muffin's injuries, so that as she was beginning to sink to the ground they caught her.

Making Muffin as comfortable as possible on the ground; Vincent, Mum and Pops looked her wounds over carefully. The villagers, gypsies and new cat warrior friends gathered around them in a circle to see if they might be able to lend assistance. For amongst them were several healers. Vincent, Mum and Pops having cleaned Muffin's wounds as best as they could allowed the healers to come forward to examine her. Muffin throughout this was calm thanking everyone for taking care of her. After the healers had inspected her wounds, they then talked amongst themselves about what could be done. Coming forward as one the healers addressed everyone with Vincent, Mum and Pops by Muffin's side. The nominated spokesman for the healers somberly stated that they would not be able to repair all of the damage done, but that they would be able to tend to some of it. The spokesman for the healers also said that they had herbs and roots to help with the pain and infection.

The three Warrior Cat companions, villagers,

gypsies and new cat warrior friends were struck silent by this. So that Muffin, who's voice was not quite as loud as usual was clearly heard as she spoke, "These healers are the best I could ever hope for. Together with my three beloved Warrior Cat companions and so many friends, my life is rich in your love. Thank you. Please come forward healers and use your knowledge on me."

A more comfortable pallet was made for Muffin. A fire was lit so that water could be heated. While the healers readied their potions, the villagers began cooking food for the hungry from provisions they had brought with them. The gypsies were in charge of collecting wood for the fire and bringing in more water, which was needed for the healers to clean Muffin's wounds, make potions, drinking and food. All of this was done quickly, while Vincent, Mum and Pops stayed with Muffin, while the healers soon set to work deftly tending to her.

Muffin for her part began telling stories. Everyone gathered around as close as they could to listen. No one present had ever seen anything like it. For while the healers were cleaning, stitching what they could and otherwise inflicting some pain as they worked on Muffin to try to help her, The Muffin told story after story. Many of the tales were hilarious! Much laughter was heard. With Vincent, Mum and Pops laughing the loudest as she spun her tales. If it were not for all witnessing The Muffin being cared for by the healers, one would have imagined that she was just sitting round the campfire at a feast making merry! Sometimes Muffin shared a poignant story with so much passion that all who were present had eyes that glowed with unshed tears.

The healers were in awe of her, feeling very honored and fortunate to administer healing to such a rare and fine soul. At last the healers having applied their poultice to her wounds for pain and infection were done. Muffin who had just finished a story, looked upon each healer in turn grasping their hand as she expressed her gratitude for all that they had done for her. Then with her eyes sweeping over all who were present, Muffin now with Vincent, Mum and Pops by her side gave a spirited speech to all of her wonderful friends. Ending it with all of the love and thanks she could give them. Then turning to Vincent, Mum and Pops, Muffin said with a smile, "Let's go home!"

So it was with all of their gossamer dream world friends gathered near that Vincent, with Muffin gently held in his arms and Mum and Pops standing on either side of him made their fare-thee-wells. None of the four companions wanted to say a complete goodbye. Muffin who knew that she had not long on this earth but was happy to be going home called out, "There are no goodbyes among friends! Only until we meet again. May your path always be gentle upon your feet and may the wind always be at your back!" Eyes glowing with love and huge smiles on everyone's faces, Vincent standing tall carried The Muffin, with Mum and Pops on either side of him as they turned and began walking towards the golden haze.

Just before they reached it their gossamer dream world friends began chanting, "Muffin the Greatest Warrior Cat of them all. Muffin the Greatest Warrior Cat of them all and her three Warrior Cats!" Then chanting, "Muffin, Muffin, Vincent, Vincent, Mum, Mum, Pops, Pops!" Vincent with Muffin in his arms, Mum and Pops on either side of him were in front of the golden haze now. Backs to the gossamer dream world that held so many dear friends, each raised a hand to acknowledge this wonderfully grand gesture.

Then Muffin suddenly said, "Please put me down Vincent. I came into this gossamer dream world on my own and would now like to make the journey back through the golden haze in the same way." Vincent, with great care set The Muffin on her feet. Then the four companions lined up in the order that they had come into the gossamer dream world. Muffin, then Vincent, then Mum, then Pops. Their friends were beside themselves now cheering! On this note Muffin the Greatest Warrior Cat of them all and her three Warrior Cat companions let out massive roars, running as one through the golden haze towards home...

With a suddenness that belied the gossamer dream world they had just came from, a world where each day is the length of a lifetime, Muffin, Vincent, Mum and Pops emerged through the golden haze and were all at once home again. Standing in the Walnut Grove of their homeland and so much like the Walnut Grove the four had just came from, Muffin, Vincent, Mum and Pops looked around in wonder. Their lives had been so enriched by the gossamer dream world. All felt that what they had learned while being there could be used to great advantage in their own world. Smiling at one another the four opened their arms joining together in a huge hug. Then Vincent looking at his watch exclaimed in astonishment, "Do you realize we've only been gone four days which is 96 hours in our time?" "Or" Muffin said with a smile, "Four lifetimes."

NO END AND NO BEGINNINGS AND NO GOODBYES

The sun shone slowly through, then gradually rose until it was up above the huge beautiful Cedar tree in the Walnut Grove of the fours' homeland. Vincent, Mum and Pops were standing beneath its glorious branches telling stories about Muffin. These tales were sometimes hilarious, some were of bravery in battle and some were so bittersweet that their eyes glowed. These wondrous stories were told with the three of them standing side by side in front of the resting place they had made for their beloved Muffin.

None of them could believe it had been a year now since she had passed from their lives. And yet Muffin's rare and fine soul still flowed in and around Vincent, Mum and Pops. Her spirited passion for life giving them wings on which the three soared. So Muffin you see was yet still with Vincent, Mum and Pops in a bond that could never be broken and all three were most grateful for this.

Vincent who had returned after Muffin's passing to the gossamer dream world, had let their many friends there know about her. Vincent had been told that they still felt Muffin's presence amongst them and felt very fortunate. Before he returned home, Vincent was informed by their new cat warrior friends of outlying enemy cat warriors who were gathering in bands. That upon the three Warrior Cats next journey to the gossamer dream the enemy cats planned to challenge them in battle. "When you return, let us all join forces and fight these enemy cat warriors together!" said their new cat warrior friends. "And so it will be." Vincent replied before making his journey back home through the golden haze again.

Now they all three stood together at Muffin's resting place under the huge beautiful Cedar tree. With momentos from each one of them bestowed upon it, the three Warrior Cat companions told Muffin of their upcoming journey to the gossamer dream world and of the enemy cat warriors. As they finished telling her of this, light and color began to swirl around them in an incredible array of rainbow colors. It surrounded Vincent, Mum and Pops until it was a clear and glowing aura of Muffin. But not only that, but of Muffin the Greatest Warrior Cat of them all! Vincent, Mum and Pops excited had huge grins on their faces. For the message from Muffin was clear, she was going back thru the golden haze with them to do battle with these enemy cat warriors!

Vincent, his eyes shining said, "Are you ready for this Muffin?" In response Muffin's aura danced up and down excitedly. "O.k. Let's go!" Vincent, Mum and Pops sang out. Lining up like they always had, Muffin, Vincent, Mum and Pops made their way through the golden haze together. Arriving back in the gossamer dream world the four Warrior Cat companions greeted the villagers, gypsies and new cat warrior friends happily. Everyone was overjoyed to see them and talked much with the four companions. They were also told of the swift approach of the enemy cat warriors. There was much visiting while keeping a close eye out for enemy cats. Their new cat warrior friends gathered close in around the four Warrior Cat companions as they waited.

Suddenly there they were, the enemy cat warriors with their leader in front calling out the challenge and then throwing down the gauntlet to do battle. In that moment, Muffin the Greatest Warrior Cat of them all who's aura even the enemy cat warriors could see, rose up with Vincent, Mum and Pops beside her. With their new cat warrior friends at their backs, her aura now dancing she lead her three Warrior Cat companions and new cat warrior friends into battle with a roar that seemed to come from everywhere.

Her aura was so intense that Muffin's roars were heard by all. The enemy cat warriors were bewildered by these roars that seemed to come from all around them. So much so that as Muffin the Greatest Warrior Cat of them all, her three Warrior Cats and new cat warrior friends began their battle with the enemy cat warriors, some of the enemy cats were tripping over themselves trying to flee instead of fight. The enemy cats that remained seemed unable to comprehend what they were seeing. For not only was Muffin's aura sending out roars that surrounded the enemy cats, but if an enemy cat got too close to her aura, Muffin the Greatest Warrior Cat of them all would beckon them to do battle with her. Oh she was amazing to watch!

Vincent, Mum and Pops who were right beside Muffin, felt the power once more of being in battle with her. Adding their roars to hers, lined up side by side Muffin the Greatest Warrior Cat of them all and her three Warrior Cats went head long into battle with such artistry and cunning that the remaining enemy cat warriors were overwhelmed. Their new cat warrior friends were lending great effort to the battle as well. As if by mutual agreement, the enemy cat warriors realized they had bitten off more than they could chew. Turning tail the enemy cats made a fast retreat with some limping as they went.

It was then that Muffin the Greatest Warrior Cat of them all, her aura shining brightly, and her three Warrior Cats came together in unison. With light and color swirling around them, Muffin, Vincent, Mum and Pops let out massive roars. Their laughter and smiles a tribute to one another. In that moment they knew without a shadow of a doubt that no matter what they would always be there for one another. Muffin had proved just that. There was no end and no beginnings and no goodbyes. Muffin, her aura glowing with a luminous brilliance, looked into the eyes of Vincent, Mum and Pops with a huge smile on her face and once again said, "Let's go home!"

EPILOGUE

The full moon shone brightly on the Walnut Grove with its huge beautiful Cedar tree like a focal point amongst them. An amazing amount of light cast from it and shone almost like a beacon beneath the Cedar tree onto Muffin's resting place there. Vincent, Mum and Pops were sitting around a campfire in the Walnut Grove under the moonlit night sky. They had been telling stories of old and stories of new. The campfire flamed up intense colors of blue, yellow, orange and red. Shadows danced away from the circle of light that the fire created, along with the shadows that played peek-a-boo in the moon's dance with the trees. It was all together a magnificent night to commune with the spirits of loved ones and to give a toast to them in gratitude.

Vincent, Mum and Pops loved to do this on a night when the moon and campfire could dance with the shadows in the trees. This was indeed a perfect night and so they told boisterous tales of Muffin the

Greatest Warrior Cat of them all and her three Warrior Cats. They would let out wild yowls at times and dance around the campfire.

As the fire died down Vincent, Mum and Pops spoke more quietly about the grand adventures they had with Muffin in the gossamer dream world and in their homeland. The three then rose as one walking over to the huge beautiful Cedar tree. Moonbeams of light cast like glittering diamonds beneath its limbs. Iridescently it shone on Muffin's resting place there. As Vincent, Mum and then Pops ducked to go under the Cedar trees' limbs, the moonbeams of brilliant light danced beneath it drawing them in until they stood side by side almost touching the dancing moonlight.

Watching more closely now, Vincent, Mum and Pops became aware of these iridescent moonbeams moving and dancing around until suddenly Muffin's image shone luminously smiling at them. She came to them every so often, especially on a night like tonight. Muffin always seemed to know when Vincent, Mum and Pops needed a boost of her Warrior Cat strength. The magnitude of her power washed over them like a healing balm. They smiled back at her, each of them reaching out a hand towards her. In return, Muffin's luminous image reached out a paw touching them not just spiritually but also physically as well. This was an amazing phenomenon. Something more precious to Vincent, Mum and Pops than the finest of jewels.

As they expressed their love for her, Muffin's image danced until she was out from beneath the Cedar tree and over near the campfire. They rushed after her back over to the fire. Vincent added more wood building it up until it blazed brightly. Then Muffin, Vincent, Mum and Pops smiled tremendously at one another as they began to dance with great abandon around the fire. Cat Dances...Moon Dances...

AFTERWORD

Vincent, Mum and Pops still go forth each day in the spirit of Muffin. Sharing their otherworldly knowledge to all who are open to it. They still dance with Muffin every chance they get. Be it in their homeland or the other world thru the golden haze. Living their lives as if in a gossamer dream where each day is the length of a lifetime...

ABOUT THE AUTHOR

Jude Bales is a singer-songwriter who has been writing songs since the age of twelve. This is her first creative non-fiction book. Jude lives with her husband on the 38th parallel north. She is currently at work on a collection of childhood stories.

www.ingramcontent.com/pod-product-compliance
Lightning Source LLC
Chambersburg PA
CBHW060749050426
42449CB00008B/1328